Table of Contents

DISCLAIMER

The publisher has put forth its best efforts in preparing and arranging this book. The information provided herein by the author is provided "as is" and you read and use this information at your own risk. There is no guarantee that you will get any results or financial gain from the ideas and strategies contained in this book. You alone are responsible for your successes in business and in life. The publisher and author disclaim any liabilities for any loss of profit or commercial or personal damages resulting from the use of the information contained in this book.

PREFACE

The truth is, I never envisioned myself writing a book on the business of bridal makeup artistry. When I first began my journey toward becoming a makeup artist, I couldn't picture myself in any other line of work. Once I took that first step toward what I knew had to be my career, I wanted to bleed mascara and live to share my creative talents with other women.

It wasn't easy at first. As a novice artist, I scoured the internet, looking for any tidbit that would bring me closer to becoming a professional makeup artist. I had finished college and there was no budget left for a makeup school program, so I had to forge ahead on my own.

Fast forward five whirlwind years. Since my determined and enthusiastic beginning, I've worked with hundreds of brides and freelanced in the world of fashion and advertising. My company has won awards based on customer satisfaction and I feel a great sense of accomplishment, especially because I figured it all out along the way.

As my wedding makeup company has expanded, I've added many young artists to my team and, in choosing them, I've recognized a common theme among the resumes that come my way. While many talented people have the skill and passion for the beauty industry, so many lack the business skills to create a foundation on which to build a solid career.

All too often, when looking through my inbox to choose potential new hires, I've wanted to put my arms through my computer, shake these young artists by the shoulders and ask, "What are you *thinking* with a resume like this? How can you *possibly* be planning for a successful future for your artistry business when you present yourself so carelessly?"

Given the lack of helpful information available to novice artists, I can sympathize. Most makeup academies tantalize students with claims of bright lights and exotic careers to be enjoyed while jet setting around the world with makeup brushes in hand. Unfortunately, the majority of these schools offer little in the way of actual career guidance.

That's my motivation for writing this book. I want to share what I've learned about bridal artistry from a straightforward, easy to understand perspective. I hope the experiences and knowledge that have worked for me over the years can help others bring their visions for their own pursuits to life using my tried-and-true business concepts.

I encourage you to read what I've learned, then take the time to tailor these ideas to fit your career vision. I do my best to cover everything I think you'll need to know to work in the wedding industry, but only you can choose the tools you need to blaze your own trail.

Loving what you do and having a willingness to keep going, even when there are bumps in the road, are the main keys to building a sustainable career for yourself. I can share everything I've ever learned in the pages of this book, but unless you are driven by a passion for beauty and enjoy helping others feel good about who they are, you are unlikely to succeed.

Here's the good news. If the passion and motivation to be your own boss live inside your heart, there is nothing you can't learn about becoming a business-savvy makeup artist.

SECTION I:
Business Basics

CHAPTER 1: Where Artistry Can Take You

Ask twenty makeup artists how they got their start in the industry and you will hear a mélange of different stories. Some knew they were beauty mavens from a young age, unable to picture themselves doing anything else.

Others may have come from a design background and applied that experience toward their artistry. Also, as with many careers, some happened to fall into it simply by chance or process of elimination.

No matter how they got started, any artist who continues in the business will tell you makeup artistry is a rewarding means of self-employment that enables you to help others feel confident and perhaps leave your mark on the world of beauty.

The world of makeup artistry offers many avenues to explore. Maybe you'd like to focus on the world of high fashion runway. Possibly a film and TV career would suit you best. Perhaps your unique gift is an ability to make celebrities look gorgeous as they walk down the red carpet.

Take your time. Evaluate the opportunities that beckon you along each path and truly feel out which is right for you.

If you don't find yourself interested in moving to Los Angeles, New York, Milan or one of the other fashion capitals of the world, bridal makeup artistry is one sector of the beauty industry that can lead you into a financially stable career in your own backyard, wherever that happens to be.

According to a 2012 survey conducted by the XO Group, "The average wedding budget in The US in 2012 was $28,427 with wedding budgets continuing to rise to an all-time high since 2008."

What does this mean for you, as an artist? Couples are spending more today than they ever have on this once-in-a-lifetime experience. Brides want to look amazing for their walk down the aisle – and they are willing to pay you a pretty penny for your ability to make that happen.

Often, successful makeup artists working in the entertainment or fashion industry will say, "I don't do bridal." The wedding industry is known for unnecessary stress, emotional drama and fodder for reality TV. The truth is, most bridal artists do not get the credit they deserve for their ability to create flawless beauty in this often-emotional work environment.

Just think about it. How many people can say they see someone cry *every* time they go to work? If you've ever watched a mother help her daughter get into her wedding dress, or seen a bride's reaction when she receives a love note from her groom the morning of the ceremony, you know exactly what I'm talking about.

As part of the beauty team, you are expected to provide, not *just* your artistic beauty services, but also a calming energy to help the bride be at her best throughout the most surreal day of her life. You are not only an artist, but a self-esteem builder as well. The better you understand the nature of every aspect of the job, the happier your clients will be with your services.

Providing such a unique service means you are able to charge rates that can ensure your ability to enjoy the lifestyle you've envisioned for yourself. Don't be surprised when the mother of the bride – the woman who gave you all *kinds* of trouble about the shade of her lipstick needing to match her dress *perfectly* – hands you a sizeable tip upon your exit.

While the demands of the job require you to be both flexible and thick-skinned, you will be generously rewarded, both personally and financially, if you take the steps laid out for you in this book.

CHAPTER 2: Benefits of the Job

Whether you are just looking for some extra part-time income or seeking a full-fledged career in makeup artistry, working in the wedding industry is a rewarding career. Let's face it, how many jobs out there make it possible to help a woman feel beautiful on what is deemed the most important day of her life?

As bride stylists, our presence in the bridal suite has one purpose – to make sure the bride feels confident and beautiful when she walks down the aisle. While the job certainly has its stresses, the wedding industry can be very lucrative for a talented artist who brings a strong marketing strategy and vision to the business, right along with artistic talent and people skills.

Every day you go to work will be different. Every bride you meet, every mother who watches over your work and every venue you travel to will deliver a new set of circumstances. One of the best aspects of the job is the opportunity you will have to meet so many unique and fascinating women along the way.

Nearly all of us have experienced the caged feeling that arises as we count the minutes until we are freed from a cubical for the day. If you struggle with the concept of a desk job, on-location aspect of the artistry business is your perfect alternative to staring at the clock all day.

As in any business, there are certainly pros and cons to owning your own makeup artistry business, but cons are far outweighed by the true benefits of owning a bridal beauty company.

Perks of the Wedding Industry
The colorful nature of the wedding business makes it fair to say you will never be bored. No two clients are alike and each bridal party will bring you a variety of experiences.

Some bridesmaids will pop the champagne cork at 10 a.m. and throw a dance party, causing you to ask yourself if you work in a nightclub. Others will quietly eat breakfast and sleepily wait for their turn in the chair.

As a self-employed artist, you make your own schedule. Don't feel like working on a holiday? No longer can your boss force you to work while others play. Of course, it *is* wise to consider offering higher "holiday rates" to brides who decide to get married on these days.

You are your own boss . . . well sort of. The truth is each client is your real boss. Nevertheless, you decide how your company runs and what services you offer. The only quotas you have to meet are the goals you've set yourself to achieve.

Artists often work far fewer hours than people with regular jobs, most can't remember the last time they worked a forty-hour workweek. Don't be surprised if what you make from a wedding in one day matches or exceeds your weekly take home pay from your old job.

The business of makeup artistry involves studying the latest trends in bridal fashion and keeping abreast of new product technology and releases. All seriousness aside, this is *fun*. No artist will ever complain about having to stay on top of what the hottest designers are doing or scoping out new products that will help them do a better job.

For makeup addicts, the ability to justify spending thousands on makeup over the course of your career is pure bliss. After all, without a properly stocked makeup kit one cannot be prepared to beautify any face they encounter. Makeup purchases in the name of preparedness are just plain smart.

As a freelance artist, you choose your clients, unlike most customer service positions, where employees are forced to grin and bear it while being faced with a difficult client. Fortunately for you, you will soon learn to recognize those red flags that pop up as a dead giveaway for bridezillas. Suddenly, you will already be booked for their wedding day. So sorry.

Another perk? You can work with your best friends. As your business grows and you find yourself needing extra help, why not hire people you like? The energy your team brings to the bridal suite will be so much more upbeat if you work with your friends.

As I spout off about all the benefits of being a makeup artist, I am aware that you know most of this already. The benefits of the job may be clear, but the path to achieving them is not always so easy.

How many tacky, bedazzled, outdated makeup artist websites have you come across? In my years of working in the industry I have certainly seen some very poorly executed artistry businesses. The bad news is that talent and artistry skills are the easy part of your business. After all, your artistic talent is a gift.

The difficult task is laying down a path to success based on combining that talent with a sound business plan. Thankfully, all of this can be taught. If you are only looking for extra-income and don't find yourself committed to building a freelance career, many great opportunities are available for you as well.

Options are plentiful with spas, hotels, or another full-time bridal company. Decide on the path that feels right for you, the one that lights you up with passion and motivation to succeed.

CHAPTER 3: Structuring Your Artistry Business

By now, you have started to think about your dream career and feel ready to take the first exciting step toward building your beauty business. The first thing you need to do is choose a business structure that will dictate how your company operates and how the government will recognize you.

The three main options are: sole proprietorship, LLC (Limited Liability Company), and S or C corporation. Most artists elect to operate as a sole proprietorship, but let's explore these options a little further.

Sole Proprietorship

This is the artist's simplest, most commonly chosen method of business operation. The sole proprietorship itself does not function as a legal entity. Its purpose is to recognize that you own the business and you are responsible for the company's debts.

If you choose this route for your bridal company, you can operate under your own name or choose a fictitious business name (commonly known as a DBA – doing business as).

Only you can decide whether being a sole proprietor is the best fit for your situation. The sole proprietorship is popular because it is simple to set up and the associated costs with this business structure are low.

The unique disadvantage of operating as a sole proprietorship is that you, as owner, are personally liable for the business's debts and any lawsuits that may be brought against the company. That means, if you were to lose in a lawsuit brought against your company, you would be personally responsible for payment.

Setting up a sole proprietorship is a simple process. Generally, the only requirements are to register your name and secure a local tax license.

LLC
LLC or Limited Liability Company formation has become very popular among small business owners because, similar to a corporation, an LLC protects the owner from the threat of personal liability when it comes to lawsuits and any debts carried by your business.

By choosing to structure your company as an LLC, you also avoid the double taxation that corporations experience. This is typically the favorite choice for small businesses with one to three owners.

Are you considering teaming up with a hairstylist friend or fellow makeup artist? An LLC may be your smartest choice.

S or C Corporation
Without going into too much boring detail, the perks of operating as a corporation are based primarily on pass-through taxation and limited personal liability. That means that, as you report the earnings and losses of your wedding company on your individual tax return, you pay taxes at a personal rate instead of the corporation (your company's) net earnings.

If you live outside The United States, it is worthwhile to do online research regarding small business structures in your chosen locale to evaluate your options. Also, consider consulting a local attorney to discuss the best options for your financial needs and protections.

DBA
DBA means, "doing business as," and refers to operating under a fictitious business name, which means any name other than your legal name. For instance, if your name is Melissa Darling but you conduct business under the name of Darling Makeup Artistry, you may be required to register the business's fictitious name with your local county clerk.

Laws vary from state to state, so check the website of your county to learn what is required of you in order to file your company's paperwork. In addition, some states require each new business owner to place an ad in a local newspaper stating the new name you will be using.

Prices for these ads can vary widely from paper to paper, so do your homework. For example, I paid just $18 to run my company's ad in a small local newspaper for 90 days.

If you will be conducting business under a fictitious name, it is important to have this step done before you go to a local bank to get started with your business banking. Banks often require you to present your DBA certificate from the county office when you open a business checking account.

Liability Insurance

Since you are the creative type and spend your time dreaming of fashion and beauty, the last thing you are probably concerned with is liability insurance to protect your assets.

If you do have assets (valuable things that you own) on your balance sheet, you should strongly consider purchasing a policy to protect you from potential claims made against you.

If you live in the US, you can't help but take notice of the litigious state of our nation. A scorned client could potentially bring a lawsuit against you, regardless of how ridiculous their claim may seem.

From claims of personal injury to poor performance resulting in damages, the unfortunate reality is that these lawsuits happen all the time, and it's always best to protect yourself.

If you are a young starving artist with nothing but dreams and a well-stocked makeup kit, very few lawyers would consider taking on a case against you. However, if you own a home or have considerable financial assets, you should strongly consider a liability policy.

CHAPTER 4: Taxes Simplified

It's a fact. Coming up with a way to talk about taxes that won't be mind numbing for you, the reader, is about as challenging as taxes themselves. These brief details will help put you in the best position to set yourself up for success when tax season rolls around.

The consensus is that, as a self-employed individual, you should set aside approximately 30% of your monthly income in a tax savings account.

The combination of federal, state and self-employment taxes can be considerably higher than what you've paid in the past as an employee, so it's smart to be prepared when tax time comes around. Plus, if you have a little extra in your account after you pay those taxes, you're ahead of the game!

One of the smartest things a makeup artist can do is to open a savings account specifically for tax payments when you go to the bank to set up a business checking account. Allocating your money as soon as it you make a deposit can save you from having to come up with the funds to cover a hefty tax bill at the end of the year.

Many artistic people struggle with the accounting aspect of owning a business. You have the chance to do yourself a big favor by setting your accounts up correctly right from the beginning.

Remember, when it comes to taxes, it is your responsibility to understand the laws and make payments accordingly. The IRS is not a fan of excuses and could take legal action against you if they suspect you of fraud.

Tip: Check with your bank to see if you can set up automatic deposits to your tax savings account.

Deductions

One of the biggest perks self-employment brings you – aside from doing what you love to do – is the ability to deduct your expenses from your annual income. To do this correctly, it is important to keep accurate receipts of any item you plan to deduct. It's easy to stay on top of this if you make a weekly habit of sitting down with your accounting software to track your expenses.

Once you've recorded your deductions in your accounting software program, file the receipts category. Consider using a mini-recipe file folder labeled by expense category.

You can deduct almost everything you spend specifically on your business. Think about the tools of your trade – all those makeup products. Also, advertising costs, meals while on the job, home office expenses, and even the mileage from driving to and from wedding jobs, can all offset your tax bill.

Hiring An Accountant

At the beginning, your taxes may look relatively simple, but it's best to go to a tax accountant and have a professional review your taxes. They can give you sound advice based on your overall financial picture and guide you in setting your future financial goals and savings targets.

Although online tax software, such as TurboTax, has come a long way since its inception, tax software can never replace the specific advice you get from a professional accountant. Plus, the fees you will pay may very well be deductible too!

Estimated Payments

As a self-employed artist living in The United States, you will most likely need to make quarterly tax payments to The IRS. Payments are to be equal in size and based on your previous year's income. Consult your accountant to discuss your best options.

CHAPTER 5: Start-up Costs

That's about it for the basic legalities of getting started as a professional bridal makeup artist. Now, it's time to talk about the tangible things you'll need to get started.

Fortunately, a makeup artist's start-up costs are relatively low compared to those of many other career fields. You can expect to spend approximately $1,500-$2,000 USD to get your business off the ground.

As a novice artist, you'll be building your career as you go, so it's perfectly fine to spread your purchases over a period of time. If you decide to make your purchases gradually, it is wisest to hold off on operating as a professional makeup artist until you have accumulated all of the things you'll need to run your business.

The last thing you want to do is to put yourself in the position of looking like an amateur in front of people who can refer wedding jobs your way and risk damage to your reputation.

Makeup Kit
First things first. You will need a makeup kit that enables you to create a wide variety of looks on all ethnicities. You may think you are familiar with the look of your primary customer, but the truth is that you have to expect to encounter the unexpected. The bride who hired you may have a bridesmaid who was her college roommate…and an international student.

Fill your makeup kit with an arsenal of products that will help you deliver the wow factor – no matter the client's ethnicity. Any girl who has ever applied mascara can call herself an amateur artist. That's not you! As a professional artist, you have the ability to create exceptionally beautiful looks on the face of anyone who lands in your chair.

Beyond the basic items that go in your makeup kit, do not overlook the ones that need constant replenishment, such as eyelashes and disposable applicators.

You will need a professional makeup hard case or suitcase for your makeup kit, preferably one with wheels. I recommend using a hard shell suitcase that you can purchase from the luggage department at discount stores. These suitcases can cost hundreds less than "professional makeup cases" and, ultimately, they offer the same protection.

Stay away from Caboodles and small train cases designed for personal makeup. Those are commonly used by amateurs and *your* two-fold focus is on presenting yourself professionally while protecting the investment you've made in your kit.

Tip: Keep your personal makeup separate from your professional makeup kit. There's no need to share your bacteria with your clients.

Website & Marketing
Your annual cost to maintain a marketable website will start at about $100 and go up from there based on your hosting plan and design. A free website will *not* be suitable to represent a professional makeup artist, so please don't even consider going that route. This is one mistake amateurs make, while the purpose of this book is to guide you toward starting a professional artistry business.

Your website is no place to cut corners. It is your primary marketing tool and the way you represent yourself to potential bride clients. It would be better to work a second job to earn the money to buy a killer website that highlights your talents and sets you apart from the competition. Ultimately, the extra effort and expense will be more than worth it.

When you are ready to think about your marketing plan and how you'll get brides to find you, it's time to consider your annual advertising budget. Difficult to estimate, the costs will vary based on the size of your business and where you're located.

Remember – it is essential to have skin in the game if you expect to be seen by potential brides. The more they see your company's name, the more likely they are to hire you.

Other Start-up Costs

One of your most valuable tools an artist can have is a smart phone equipped with GPS that enables you to easily find the venue or home where you will be working. The wedding business has no room for being late. The beauty team works first on the big day, and the entire wedding schedule can be thrown off by a makeup artist who couldn't find their way to work. *Don't be that person!*

Every business needs a way to track the in-and-out flow of money, and free bookkeeping software for your new business can be found online. Also, the world we live in is constantly transitioning away from cash, so you will need to be able to accept electronic payments. Depending on the payment methods you choose to accept, transactions are free, while a small percentage is deducted from each sale (example: PayPal).

Don't Forget Emergency Savings

Beginning a life of self-employment can be one of the most exhilarating steps you can take, but you'll enjoy it more if you're wise enough to start your journey with a few months' worth of living expenses in your personal savings account.

Even if you're among the most dedicated of artists, it will take a couple of years to grow your company to the point where you are satisfied with your financial earnings.

Avoid stress and worry during slow times by keeping a reserve of cash on hand to cover needs as they arise. Saving money isn't always easy. Consider working a second job to help make ends meet while you're building your business. There is no shame in doing what it takes to ensure your own success.

CHAPTER 6: Writing an Artistry Business Plan

Why Write One?

When it comes to whether or not you need a business plan, there are a multitude of different opinions. Once you decide to do so, you can choose from dozens of different business plan styles.

Consider writing a business plan that will outline your financial goals, set benchmarks for where you would like your wedding business to take you and list your action steps toward achieving those goals.

The best way to make your business plan work for you is to realize that it is a constant work in process that you update over time. A year from now, you may have a completely different perspective on your wedding company's goals. Scrapping ideas that didn't work and replacing them with new strategies designed to reach more brides is an integral part of being a business owner.

When to Write Your Plan

Picture this. I was just starting out as a makeup artist and just *thinking* about building a business felt like an insurmountable task. After all, I was just learning to be an artist. To keep things from feeling overwhelming, the process of writing your business plan should coincide with the development of your makeup artistry skills.

That way, from the infancy stages of your business, you can begin researching your bridal market and look clearly at your financial picture. Don't be afraid to get started, even if you don't have the slightest idea where to begin.

Take your time to work through the process and you will be able to develop a solid plan, factoring in all the variables of your particular bridal market. Start slow and test your ideas over time, and you can minimize the risk of making bad business decisions.

Dream up your plan. Then, map out your action steps and test them. As you learn what works and what doesn't, go back to the drawing board. This is how every successful company operates.

What Should Be Included In Your Plan
If you are developing the plan just for yourself, rather than trying to raise money from investors or relatives, you don't need a lengthy plan. The most important thing is that you have clearly defined your goals and the steps you will take to reach them. You'll want to include:

- Mission statement for your company
- Description of services
- Market analysis of your local bridal market
- What makes you different from your competitors
- How you will market your services to brides
- Future opportunities for expansion
- A cash flow statement
- Revenue projections
- Six-month, one-year and two-year goals

For more resources and great writing tips visit the Small Business Administration's website at www.sba.gov

CHAPTER 7: Contracts

Would you believe it that the stability and permanence of your wedding company depends on the strength of one single document? Your service contract ensures your job security by serving as your bridal client's commitment to hire you for their wedding day services and protects you in the event that things don't go as planned.

It may sound like an intense approach to conducting business with your brides, but almost all wedding vendors sign contractual agreements with their clients.

A strong contract outlines the services that will take place on the wedding day and describes what will happen in the event of a cancellation. It also covers what will happen if you are unable to perform on the day of the wedding or if anyone is hurt as a result of your services.

As the creative type, legal formalities are the last thing on your mind, but please trust that a properly worded contract can save you an enormous amount of trouble if things do not go as smoothly as you had planned.

As your company grows in popularity and the number of weddings you are a part of increases, so does the likelihood that you will run into one or more of these unfortunate scenarios.

The best thing you can do to ensure the longevity of your business is to cover all of your bases and protect your personal assets. It is in your best interest to hire a local attorney to write a contract that complies with your local laws.

In addition to the following topics, your attorney can include specific clauses in your wedding service contract that adhere to your area's local laws.

Contract Basics

- Name and address of responsible party (bride)
- Where beauty services are to be completed
- Time frame for delivery of beauty services
- Total number of beauty services (i.e., number of bridesmaids, flower girls, mothers, etc.).
- Deposit requirements to reserve the wedding date
- Total amount due
- When full payment will be due
- Your cancellation policy
- The importance of all party members being on time
- What will happen in the event of an artist emergency
- Indemnification/limitation of liability
- The bride's signature and your signature

SECTION II:
Developing Your Talents

CHAPTER 8: Your Artistic Talents

If your love of artistry, fashion and all things beauty lead you toward a career in makeup artistry, I'm sure you'll find that the greatest reward of the job will be helping women feel beautiful.

If you are like me, you first discovered your love of makeup and the way it can enhance a woman's looks by having fun experimenting with your own face. The biggest hurdle you will face as you transition into professional artistry is the jump from working on the face in the mirror to those of paying clients.

Whether you have received classroom education in beauty application techniques, honed your skills at a department store beauty counter or are completely self-taught; the most important thing you can do is practice your craft.

As with many artistic mediums, there is something downright thrilling in discovering new sources of inspiration, learning new techniques and bringing ideas to life with the stroke of your brush.

No matter how you acquired your basic education in makeup, be prepared to spend years developing your inner artist. You may already be a makeup maven capable of delivering any look your brain can conceive on your own face; however, developing those creative talents for financial gain is a different process.

A certain level of maturity and humility is required of anyone considering a career in bridal artistry work. Remember that a woman's wedding day is considered to be the most important day of her life, and she is often at her most insecure when she meets you for the first time at her preview session.

Your job is to consult with her about the photos she has given you, listen to her ideas and use your creative talents to bring those ideas to life for her in a way that she realizes is better than she could ever have imagined.

Sounds easy, right? It's not. In a perfect world, we would easily wow our clients with the simple flick of an eyeliner pencil or the perfect shade of red lipstick the second they pick up the mirror. When you are ready to face reality, prepare yourself to handle insecurities, indecision, and even criticism with delicacy and tact.

Common feedback from brides will require you to be extremely patient, but if you can handle her concerns with confidence and respond knowledgeably, you can reassure her that she looks ten times prettier than she thinks she does.

Be ready. You'll hear: "I like nude, but is it the right *shade* of nude?" "Can you make my eyes look bigger and my cheeks not so fat?" "I want to look natural." These types of concern will arise from even the nicest clients. Respond encouragingly and wow her with your ability to make her feel beautiful.

Bridal makeup artistry is not for the thin-skinned. It is essential that you take every opportunity to get your hands on as many faces as possible before taking on your first paying bride client.

Entering the market too soon could do great damage to your reputation because, as you will soon find out, the number of wedding professionals, in even the largest cities, is rather small.

Take time to develop your makeup skills like any commercial artist would do. Be humble throughout your learning process and remember that even the most difficult client can present learning opportunities.

CHAPTER 9: Self-Learning Tools

As someone interested in learning the ropes of professional makeup artistry, you are constantly being bombarded with advertising messages about how to become and succeed as a makeup artist.

If you read the biographies of the world's top makeup artists, you will learn that few of them have any formal education in makeup artistry. Most of them focused instead on apprenticing with established artists or honing their skills at beauty counter jobs.

As with most trades, hands-on learning is nearly always the best, whether it comes through formal instruction or just having at it. If you decide to take your education into your own hands, here is some advice on how to get started.

Study the Classics

Read the books of industry leaders such as Kevyn Aucoin, Bobbi Brown, Scott Barnes and other artists who inspire you. Dive in headfirst. Study their techniques and fully absorb the lessons they teach by sharing their years of experiences. It's guaranteed that you will find these books a lot more fun to read than cosmetology textbooks.

Magazines

Did you know that almost every photo shoot, no matter how exclusive or high-end, involves mood boards that illustrate the feeling they are trying to create? Or that they often pull examples from magazine editorials for inspiration? Yes, it's just like an old school version of Pinterest.

If you are you looking to practice an endless array of fashion-forward styles, fashion and beauty editorials can be your greatest muse. Pull editorials from current magazines and try to re-create those looks on yourself and your friends.

Don't stop there, though. It is very helpful to reference magazine stories in online archives from the past one hundred years. Study the beauty trends of each decade and learn to replicate these looks. It will increase the strength of your artistry ten-fold.

You never know when a vintage-loving bride will sit down in your chair. On the other hand, trendy clients can be very impressed when you have the ability to put a modern twist on a classic style.

YouTube Tutorials

The quality of instruction available on YouTube varies greatly, but there is something to be said about how-to videos that can teach techniques that you may be struggling to learn on your own. As I'm sure you've already experienced, those with an eye for beauty can tell very quickly whether they are watching a highly skilled artist or a young hobbyist.

These days, many top pros have their own dedicated YouTube channels. You have the unique opportunity to use what amounts to a free subscription to learn techniques directly from your dream mentors. These makeup artists could charge hundreds of dollars for a hands-on workshop, yet they freely offer their knowledge on YouTube.

Visit the channel of British makeup artist Lisa Eldridge. She is a brilliant mentor who shoots very high-end instructional videos. For hair, L'Oreal stylist Johnny Lavoy teaches updo techniques in a fun, easy to follow way.

Learn Ingredients and Study New Technology

The more you know about why a product works the way it does, the better your choices of what to buy and how to use it to bring out your brides' best features. Don't be afraid to nerd out on cosmetic ingredients. Your clients will thank you for being so well informed.

Thinking harder about the latest trends in beauty technology will guide you toward better purchases that save you money and help you wow your clients. Using products that "do more" will improve your profitability and make your clients feel like they are wearing less makeup. It's really a win-win.

Beyond understanding key ingredients, keep yourself informed about buzzwords in beauty products and develop a basic understanding of how to read product labels. Often, clients with allergies will ask you whether your makeup contains particular ingredients.

While the decision is ultimately yours, it's wise to avoid working with people who have known cosmetic allergies because of the potential to create problems for you, the artist, when risking the client's health.

It's not worth the extra money to potentially cause harm to a paying client or put your company in jeopardy due to a damaging lawsuit.

Practice Improves Technique
Yes, this has already been covered extensively, but the best thing you can do for your artistic development is practice your makeup artistry regularly. Test new methods and products on yourself and then ask your friends and family if they will be your model for the day.

Everyone wants to look and feel beautiful, you will have no problem finding people on whom to practice your new ideas. Ask a girlfriend if you can do her makeup before a night out or for an event she is attending.

Part of becoming a successful professional makeup artist is creating the looks your clients want. That means you don't usually get to choose the look for a paying client. It's a great idea to prepare for this when doing a friend's makeup. Ask them what *they* want to do and create looks based on their ideas.

If your only experience comes from creating looks from your own imagination or photos you have pulled, your skill set will be limited. The next time you practice on a friend or family member, have them choose a couple of photos and tell you what they like about them. From there, use your creativity to develop this style for their features.

This challenge will pay off exponentially once you take on professional work. Don't be surprised when a bride brings you photos she expects you to carbon copy on her own face.

This scenario happens all the time, regardless that it is nearly impossible to pull off. When it comes to explaining the impossibility of copying any photo exactly, it's best to be very candid with your clients.

Each face is unique, and no one knows exactly how much Photoshop has been used to achieve the beautiful face women aspire to have.

Regardless of how unrealistic brides can be, it is your job to be confident in creating looks based on other people's visions for themselves. At the end of the day, this is where your money is.

Fresh Sources of Inspiration
Every now and then, you will receive an odd styling request (I've been asked for both Game of Thrones and Disney Princess looks), but most brides will tell you they want to look elegant and timeless on their wedding day.

While bridal trends change a bit more slowly than those of the high fashion runway, each year brings new bridal beauty styles. For you, as the makeup artist, it's both fun and beneficial to maintain a constant stream of new inspiration flowing your way.

Subscribe to Blogs
Beauty and wedding blogs share the pulse of what's hot right now with their readers. Both offer windows into current trends and the ability to light your creative mind on fire with possibility.

If you are determined to be a top artist in your region, you need to know what is going on in the world of beauty and how you can create trend-worthy looks that will flatter the unique features of your clientele.

Green Wedding Shoes, Style Me Pretty, 100 Layer Cake, and Wedding Chicks are just a few outstanding blogs loaded with bridal beauty inspiration. To stay on top of new content, follow blogs with your Facebook account so that you have a feed of fresh posts that link directly to trend-worthy articles.

Follow the Red Carpet
The most popular inspiration photos brides bring to a makeup artist feature celebrities on the red carpet. These looks work very well for brides, and it is important that you keep yourself current in the latest red carpet beauty trends.

Tune into the red carpet segments of award shows. Read the best and worst dressed sections of magazines. Follow the Instagram accounts of Hollywood's biggest celebrity makeup artists, too. They often post headshots of their celebrity work even before they make it onto the carpet and sometimes mention the products they used to create the look.

Tip: Don't be afraid to comment on their photos and seek advice. You never know what you might learn!

Bridal Market Week
Keep up with Bridal Market Week (bridal fashion week) in New York. Study this event like it's your professional trade show. These runway shows presented by the industry's top designers will give you valuable insights into upcoming bridal beauty trends.

Shows often feature avante garde styles, and most brides would drop dead before wearing these dresses, but new trends are born at every show. Also featured are unique hair accessories and jewelry that you can consider selling to your clients. It can be both exciting and profitable to keep up with this year's Bridal Market Week.

Pinterest
I know. You're already completely addicted to Pinterest. You don't need my help to tell you how to use it. New beauty content becomes part of Pinterest every single day and Pinboards filled with looks you love are great for sharing with clients. Your Pinboards have the

ability to inspire ideas and show off your personal aesthetic.

Occasionally, a bride will sit down in your chair with no photos of her own in hopes that you will have a gallery of styles for her to choose from. Other times, a bride might have a hard time articulating the style she is after. Not to worry. Pull ideas from your Pinterest boards to show her that you know what she is looking for.

CHAPTER 10: Makeup School - Yes or No?

Currently, a seemingly infinite number of educational options in makeup artistry are available. From local schools to online programs, the quality of these institutions varies greatly. In truth, it is questionable whether students ever recoup the investment they make in these programs.

Unless you are able to study at one of the top makeup academies, such as Makeup Designory, Joe Blasco, or Cinema Secrets, self-study will get you exactly where you need to be.

Even if you can afford to attend one of these prestigious schools, it should only for the purpose of pursing a career in special effects film makeup. For bridal and event makeup, options learning on your own are plentiful and cost considerably less.

Determined to pursue formal education in the beauty industry? Why not consider a cosmetology program? It *is* the lengthiest option, but the payoff includes a license to legally work in a salon setting. Not to mention the additional benefit of gaining the skills to create beautiful hairstyles for weddings.

As a business owner, it's to your advantage to keep your eyes open for new opportunities to grow your company. Offering hair services will greatly enhance your value to your bride clients, increase your revenue stream, and diversify your job opportunities within the beauty industry. Don't see hairstyling in your future? Consider pairing up with a stylist or hiring a freelancer for your team.

As far as what a cosmetology program offers, most do not go into detailed makeup application. As a supplement, why not further develop your craft by traveling to workshops presented by industry experts? Who doesn't want an excuse to take a trip in the name of bettering themselves?

In lieu of strictly formal education, attending makeup industry trade shows like The Makeup Show and IMATS offers workshops from top artists, and you can get your hands on products specifically for professional makeup artists. You will learn more from sitting in on Q & A seminars with these experts than spending $5,000 on a makeup instruction program.

If you do decide makeup school is the right path for you, please do extensive research on the history of the school, the experience of the instructors and where past graduates are working today *before* committing to a program.

Quality varies greatly from school to school and your investigation may reveal that some schools are reputable while damaging lawsuits are pending against others.

Beyond the cost of attending a makeup program, consider the ultimate purpose of the certificate you will receive. I hate to be the bearer of bad news, but a makeup certificate is a virtually useless piece of paper bride clients and department store jobs do not care about.

There is a big difference between a certificate of completion from a makeup academy and a cosmetology license. Find out if the laws in your area require a state cosmetology or esthetician license to perform makeup and hair services. If so, you will need to attend an accredited cosmetology or esthetics program, not a makeup academy.

Sadly, many people throw away money to earn these certificates when, as a new artist, you would be better served to take a job at a department store, honing your skills at a beauty counter. You will learn directly from a cosmetics brand, applying techniques that you will use on real women every day you go to work. This type of hands-on experience far exceeds the learning potential derived from classroom education.

CHAPTER 11: Shopping

For me, the most thrilling aspect of starting out as a new makeup artist was having an excuse to buy the best makeup I could justify adding to my cart, in every shade of color I could manage to get my hands on. The first couple years of my career were a cosmetic shopping spree of astronomical proportions.

I hate to have to admit this but, for a number of reasons, about thirty percent of my purchases from those days never touched a client's face. The colors were too dramatic. I didn't like the texture on the skin or I just didn't understand how to use it. Some of those items are still boxed up in my makeup closet with little hope of ever seeing the light of day.

Please learn from my mistakes and exercise self-control when choosing what to buy for your professional kit. It is important to review your business plan, focus on your target client and buy products that support the type of work you will be doing on a day-to-day basis.

When working with brides, you will need a kit full of beautiful, better than everyday, long-lasting makeup. That crimson red eye shadow that looks so on-trend right now? No client will ever wear it.

That tube of lilac lipstick from your most coveted brand? Put it down now. It is not tasteful, even on the most confident of bridesmaids.

Success in a makeup artistry career will come from making the most of the right products that don't break the bank. After all, you are in this business to build the life you've always imagined for yourself, not to spend years paying off credit card debt from unprofitable makeup purchases.

Shield your eyes as you walk quickly past those bold eye shadows at Sephora. You won't *ever* use them. If you know shopping in person will lead you to impulse purchases, make a conscious decision to shop online. Read product reviews and be smart about every product you allow into your shopping cart.

Here are some of the places top makeup artists shop for professional quality products that allow them to create flawless looks for their clients.

Camera Ready Cosmetics
www.crcmakeup.com
This online store carries a wide variety of professional products that will cover just about everything you could ever need as a professional artist. The staff is well versed on the products they carry, so don't be afraid to ask questions. Professional makeup artists with the proper credentials receive a discount, and they ship internationally.

Sephora
www.sephora.com
Sephora is tried and true, and they sell just about every prestige brand of makeup. You will pay full retail price for these products, but the selection is top-notch. Beauty Insider Points add up for great freebies and, as a bonus, ask for samples of products you are interested in buying. Sephora will offer you a sample of just about any product they carry. Don't be afraid to ask.

Naimie's Beauty Center
www.naimies.com
Offers a very comprehensive selection of professional makeup tools and supplies. The physical store is in Los Angeles, but you can order via email or phone with an impressive professional artist discount to those who qualify. Ships to The US and Canada.

ULTA Beauty
www.ultabeauty.com
Ulta offers you the perfect balance between high-end prestige cosmetics and the everyday brands you know and love. While you will eventually need a makeup kit loaded only with the best quality brands, when you are just starting out, it is okay to mix in drugstore brands. Sign up for the Ulta loyalty card to receive fantastic coupons every week via email. The value of these coupons can't be stressed

enough for their cost-cutting benefits.

Sally Beauty Supply
www.sallybeauty.com
Although their primary focus is hair products, Sally's has a small section of makeup disposables such as mascara wands and plastic dippers. Not the best on pricing, but Sally's can get you out of trouble if you are in a pinch when you need last-minute disposables or eyelashes before a wedding.

Madame Madeline
www.madamemadeline.com
This is a source for a very comprehensive selection of eyelashes. Their prices on individual pairs beat just about any retailer out there. When purchasing multiple pairs, you receive an even deeper discount. Make sure to read the specials section to obtain coupon codes for additional offers. Ships to The US, Canada and The UK.

CHAPTER 12: Professional Artist Discounts

Can you imagine being able to purchase makeup below retail prices just because you are a working makeup artist? It might sound like a dream come true, it is a fact that many coveted brands extend a professional artist discount program to artists with the necessary credentials. These programs will save you a fortune over the length of your career.

Before you have a heart attack trying to learn how to make it into the programs, know that it will take you some time to meet the requirements. These discount programs are a privilege not to be taken lightly. Do not try to cut corners by submitting inaccurate or falsified documents or you could be banned from the programs altogether.

Due to abuse by participants who have unlawfully resold product purchased through these programs for a profit, the rules are very strict, and many companies require you to reapply every two years.

How do you find out which brands offer professional artist discount programs? Visit the websites of your favorite brands. There, you will often find a link to a page detailing the requirements of their program. If not, search their FAQ or email customer service and ask what they offer to makeup artists.

Common Requirements

Website
A professional website in your business name with a professional portfolio and your contact information.

Magazine Tear Sheet
This term, which comes from tearing the page of the magazine you've worked on to place directly in your portfolio, refers to a

magazine editorial you have participated in that credits you as the makeup artist for the shoot. It will take time to build to level where you are doing makeup for magazine editorials, whether they are for fashion magazines or local bridal publications.

A Call Sheet with Name Credit
Used mainly in the commercial and film world, a call sheet is a daily directive from a production company listing the members of the cast and crew, detailing when and where they need to report to work. You will be listed as the makeup artist for the job.

Business Card
Your card must list your business name, contact information and clearly show your specific profession.

Professional License
This applies only to those with state registered cosmetology or esthetics licenses. Please note that this is not the same as a certificate of completion from a makeup school program. While some companies will accept such completion certificates, many will not.

Letter of Employment
A letter from your employer stating that you work for their company as a makeup artist. Most brands will not accept a letter of employment if you work as a retail artist in a department store; instead, it would need to come from the owner of an independent bridal company or salon where you perform makeup professionally.

Photo ID
Government-issued photo identification that lists your current address. In most cases, makeup brands will only ship to the address listed on the card.

CHAPTER 13: Hygiene

Did you know that studies show department store makeup samples are covered in traces of fecal matter? Have you ever heard stories of pink eye from women who've had their makeup done for an event?

Unfortunately, these scenarios are all too common. That's exactly why the importance of utilizing proper hygiene techniques cannot be stressed enough.

Clients appreciate nothing more than witnessing you take the proper steps to ensure a clean, safe experience for them. Choosing not to practice proper hygiene jeopardizes the health of your clients and, at a minimum, makes you look unprofessional.

You should be aware that you could be held liable for giving someone an infection if you neglect the proper steps to keep your makeup kit sanitary.

Proper hygiene and maintaining a sanitary workspace is the most serious aspect of our job, and it must be practiced diligently every time a client sits in your chair.

If you have ever been a student in a state-run cosmetology program you have been versed on the rules of proper hygiene inside and out. It's hopeful that makeup academy programs taught the same techniques, but the quality of education varies greatly from school to school.

At a minimum, follow these steps:

Wash your brushes *every* time they are used. No exceptions. Use baby shampoo instead of soap in hopes of preserving the life of the hair fibers. Avoid completely submerging brushes in water or the glue at the base of the fibers will begin to disintegrate.

Allow your brushes to air dry by laying them out on a towel with the fibers hanging over the edge of a counter or table. Avoid drying your brushes flat on a towel because this puts the hair fibers at risk of developing fungus or bacteria.

Always use disposable dipping wands or spatulas with products that require you to dip directly into the packaging. This includes but is not limited to: mascaras, cream or gel eyeliners and eye shadows, lipsticks, glosses, cream blushes, foundations, etc.

All creams and liquids should be scooped onto your sanitized palette, and dipped into from there as opposed to direct use from product packaging. Using a clean palette for each client keeps your kit clean and gives clients peace of mind.

Hand sanitizer is your best friend. When clients see you apply it to your hands, they know you've taken the initial steps to protect them from potentially harmful bacteria. Your fingernails should be kept short to prevent makeup from piling up underneath. Make sure your hands exude a constant aura of cleanliness.

Over the years, I have seen many artists in the bridal suite apply mascara directly from the tube onto paying clients. Nothing is more cringe-worthy than watching someone who is supposed to be a professional spread bacteria from client to client. Not only is this reckless, it is easily avoided. Purchase disposable applicators from any makeup supply store to ensure safety for your clients.

Tip: Excess powder on your brushes? Tap it off; do *not* blow on your brushes, period.

Disposables should be the first items placed in your shopping cart every time you are shopping for new product. Disposable wands protect two essential things – the health of your clients and the longevity of your business.

To avoid running out of stock with your disposable items, keep a log in a notebook, or in your phone, listing products you are low on so you don't forget to replenish your kit.

Please protect yourself, your clients and your reputation. Do not let a simple oversight result in a nasty lawsuit that could potentially bring an end to your company and tarnish your reputation.

CHAPTER 14: Gaining Experience

By now, you have spent time teaching yourself about the world of professional makeup artistry or completed some level of formal education. Congratulations to you for being ready to take that next step in your career and work to gain experience beyond the faces of your friends and family.

During this growth period, you will create some of your proudest work to date and make some of your biggest mistakes. Embrace all of it. Those successes will propel you further and your mistakes will be your greatest learning opportunities. This next stage is when it really starts to happen.

Working at a Beauty Counter
Many of the most renowned makeup artists of our time began their careers working at department store beauty counters. These jobs offer artistic training, sales skills and an opportunity to work on nearly every eye shape, nose shape and ethnicity under the sun.

There is more to be gained from six months at a beauty counter job than from years studying techniques in your spare time. Decent starting pay and product discounts are also a plus.

While most department stores do their hiring online, it's valuable to walk through the store and ask counter employees directly about job opportunities and if they enjoy working for that particular makeup line. Learn the perks for each brand and how they differ from counter to counter.

If you are granted an interview for a position, be prepared to apply makeup on a model with certain brands. If the thought of this puts you in panic mode, don't worry – most lines are focused your personality and ability to sell product.

Volunteering

Another way to develop your skills is to volunteer your services for free at a women's shelter, or for teens that cannot afford a professional stylist for the prom. Be on the lookout for community organizations where you can make a difference in someone's day by helping them feel a little bit better about themselves. You will gain insights into the true role of a makeup artist as a self-esteem builder and have opportunities to practice on more unique faces.

Assisting Other Artists

Now that you have some experience under your belt, it's time to approach makeup artists in your area to inquire about positions on their wedding team.

If hired, you will most likely start out in an entry-level position with their company. This could involve the basics such as applying moisturizer and foundation to the bridal party. Prepare to spend time washing brushes and helping the artist shine in front of her clients.

In time, as you prove your artistry and build trust, the artist you are assisting may offer you a position on her team applying makeup to bridesmaids, mothers and other members of a large bridal party that has hired her company.

The experience you gain at these jobs will prove invaluable as you learn how to work with bridal parties and gain knowledge about what it will take to build your own company.

To get the most out of your time working for another makeup artist, always be discreet and obey the rules of the artist you are working for. The world of professional makeup artists is small, and you want to put your best foot forward when taking the leap to start your own company.

Be humble and utilize this time to learn the ropes of the bridal beauty industry while always being respectful of the artist who gave you a chance.

Freebie Bride Trap

Have you seen an online ad seeking the unpaid services of an inexperienced makeup artist in exchange for the opportunity and exposure? It is best to stay far away from these "offers."

In most cases they will only leave you feeling used and frustrated. Any bride seeking free makeup services for her wedding day is likely to be a handful for you to deal with and will offer you nothing in return but a day's work without pay.

Hone your craft the right way. Build your portfolio over time and gain professional experience in ways that will eventually allow you to command a pretty penny for your services. The last thing you want is to wind up lumped in with the crowd of "low-budget artists." These people rarely find lasting success.

Your landlord is not going to accept payment in the form of "exposure." How can any artist pay the bills when they work for free or next to nothing? This *is* a business after all. Charge what you know you are worth.

SECTION III:
Bridespeak

CHAPTER 15: Communicating With Brides

Delivering perfection for clients who have been playing out their dream wedding in their head since they were six years old is no small feat. It's part fantasy, part very expensive party, and your job is to deliver on making a bride feel drop dead gorgeous for her big day. If your mission is to wow your clients, you must develop your skills as a bride whisperer.

A talented bride whisperer knows when to share an opinion and when to silently offer a tissue. Ultimately, you need to know how to read between the lines, sense her mood of the moment and respond accordingly.

This book could have easily become a tell-all on the behind-the-scenes dramas witnessed over the years, but the truth is that the majority of women are a happy ball of emotion on their wedding day.

Your Real Role
I hate to break it to you, but if you think your job as a bridal makeup artist is to sweep into the bridal suite, make everyone look beautiful and be applauded for a job well done, it's time to re-think your artistry career. As I'm sure you've observed over the course of your life, women are chock-full of insecurities and self-doubt.

Most of a bride's alleged faults would never be noticed or agreed with by another living being and live purely in her mind. Truthfully, every one of us is guilty of this and for that reason, we as artists can be understanding – within reason. On her wedding day, a bride will be relying on to you to help minimize or erase her greatest fears about her appearance.

As a beauty artist for hire, your genuine role is *not* to make women look beautiful. Instead, you are expected to make a woman feel beautiful in her own eyes. With some clients, this may seem to be the most impossible task you will encounter throughout your career.

Even the most highly skilled artists will sometimes lose clients after the preview session because the potential client wasn't satisfied with the look you've created for her.

The truth is that even if you make her look like a Hollywood bombshell on her wedding day, if she doesn't see herself as beautiful, you are unlikely to win her business. The widely shared information about how to become a bridal makeup artist focuses on how this line of work can provide steady, easy income but fails to cover this delicate topic.

Often overlooked is guidance on how to navigate the sometimes difficult path toward making women feel stunning in such a way that they see it with their own eyes on the morning of such a surreal day.

Don't be surprised if you find yourself delegating tasks to her bridal party – asking someone to get her a bottle of water or turn the music down when she needs a quiet moment to reflect on the gravity of the day. Be aware of the bride's emotions and the overall mood of the bridal suite.

You are an essential element to making sure the start of her wedding day is both fun and easy. Don't try to "check out" in your corner and just paint pretty faces. While some days might be this easy, it's important to always stay alert to what's going on around you.

Don't let reading this make you feel panicked about how to become an amazing artist who knows how to do everything right. Take a deep breath and be patient with yourself.

The only way to really learn these things is through experience. Eventually, you will be able to read your client's energy and know exactly what she needs without her having to tell you.

Start developing this skill by paying attention to what your clients say about the look you've created for them. Ask them how they are feeling. This will help you learn to recognize whether your client is looking for someone to chat with to take her mind off what's ahead, or if she needs you to be quiet so she can focus on memorizing her vows.

Some clients have trouble giving criticism even when they are unhappy with your work. Ask questions that enable you to read the tone of her voice and make changes without making her point out exactly what's wrong. This will work wonders for customer satisfaction.

CHAPTER 16: Preview Session Success

Can you imagine which part of your job will test your abilities, personal strength and patience the most? Is it the challenge of delivering beauty perfection for a woman on her wedding day? Think again. The preview session can be the most stressful and hair-pulling aspect of the job.

The way these appointments go determines whether potential brides will hire you for their wedding day. The bride's decision will be based on a combination of your abilities to make her feel beautiful and your overall personality and presentation.

Some brides may hire you blindly, based on your portfolio and reviews from past clients, but many women want to see your work in person before making a booking decision.

The objective of a preview session is to wow potential bride clients with a demonstration of how beautifully your skills can enhance their unique features. One part artistry, one part sales, this is your moment to make her feel so drop dead gorgeous that she can't wait to get that checkbook out and reserve your services for her wedding day.

Whether you are a mobile artist who will be traveling to the bride's home for the preview appointment or work at a salon space, your time with them will be much more successful if you tell the bride what to expect ahead of time. A checklist sent out before preview appointments will help the experience go smoothly for to both of you.

Suggest brides bring inspiration photos similar to what they would like their wedding day beauty look to emulate. It's also smart to mention that her face should be clean, moisturized and free of makeup.

If you are also styling her hair, it should be clean and dry. Another good suggestion is that she wear white clothing to allow her to see the makeup colors the same way she will on her wedding day.

What has experience taught me about these appointments? Preview sessions require the greatest degree of patience from you. Yes, *much* more than the wedding day itself. Brides are hiring you for your expertise and, unfortunately, many women do not know how to articulate what they want when it comes to beauty.

For instance, everyone seems to want to "look natural," and have a "soft, smoky eye." They seem unaware that this can mean just about anything. As a professional makeup artist, you'll need to learn to read what brides are *really* saying they want, not just what their words are telling you.

Ask pointed questions about why they love the photos they've brought you. Focus on asking descriptive questions that leave no room for yes or no answers.

This practice will save a lot of time and misunderstandings because, by following through on her requests, you'll be able to give her just the look she wants. She will also be impressed by the speed at which you've brought these ideas to life for her. Kudos for finishing in under an hour.

Now that you've created the initial look and are ready for her first peak in the mirror, be forewarned. During the preview session, brides will spend seemingly endless time going into detail about how they want to look on their wedding day, and it won't matter what a great job you've done for them, they will pick your work apart in seconds.

Do *not* take any of this criticism personally. Instead, understand that she is spending the price of a luxury car on her wedding day and wants everything to be perfect. For her, the icing on the cake is making jaws drop when people see how amazing she looks as she walks down the aisle.

As in any industry, the key to delivering great customer service is remembering that success is not based on what you said or did, but on how you made your client feel. Once she feels confident that she loves the look you've created for her, she will be absolutely thrilled to have you with her on her wedding day.

Note: Some artists refer to these appointments as trial sessions or initial consultations. I prefer the term "preview session" because, to me, it indicates that the appointment serves as a dress rehearsal for her wedding look, while "trial session" implies that it's nothing more than a free try-out session.

In the interests of the long-term success of your business, it is wise to charge a healthy fee for these appointments. In fact, the preview session rate should be almost as much as your wedding day pricing. Never offer to do free previews or to apply the cost toward the wedding day services.

Offering to do the preview at no charge may *sound* like a great sales pitch, but remember that these appointments are the hardest part of your job and often run two to three hours long.

As a new artist, you are likely to experience burnout in your first month of business if you choose to offer these appointments for free. Always keep an eye on your own interests and profitability.

CHAPTER 17: The Wedding Day

The goal of this chapter is to help you be successful in guiding the flow of the wedding day and delivering flawless services for your clients. Even if you've done everything perfectly up to this point, if things don't go smoothly on the wedding day, you run the risk of receiving a negative review that can harm your reputation as a wedding vendor.

By following these simple steps, you will put your best foot forward and be assured of happy clients.

Timeline
To set your company up for success on the wedding day, create a timeline in advance, review it with the bride and get her full approval. Be sure the schedule details:

Your arrival/set up time
The exact time of each bridal party member's beauty session
What time the bride needs to be in your chair
A small window of time at the end to give each person a quick touchup

When building this timeline, work backward beginning with the time the bride needs to be ready for her photos. The wedding photographer will set a time with the bride when she needs to be ready for portrait photos.

Whether you will be doing the bride's makeup and hair or only her makeup, consider finishing her makeup before she gets her hair done. This may sound counterintuitive but there is a very good reason for this.

As the morning wears on, vendors and guests will be in and out of the bridal suite. Good luck getting her lashes on and eyeliner straight while the bride is distracted – telling her florist where to put the bouquet or welcoming her great aunt who wants to give her a hug.

These moments are usually fine while doing hair, but getting her makeup finished on time will be a challenge when you are continuously interrupted. None of this is your fault, but you will be rushed to finish on time regardless.

The main advantage of establishing a beauty timeline is based on providing a clearly defined window of time to complete your services.

The timeline will protect you when bridal party members arrive late for their appointments and allows you to charge overtime fees if the schedule runs long because one or more bridesmaids were not in your chair on time. It also reassures the bride that the bridal suite won't be a beauty free-for-all the morning of her wedding.

On the flipside, it is equally imperative that you be punctual. In the high-stress world of weddings, the saying goes, "if you are on time you are late." Remember – you work first in the day.

If the schedule runs long because you failed to complete your job in sync with the timeline you created, the schedule of the entire wedding day could be thrown off.

This does not make for happy clients and puts you at risk for receiving a negative review. Leave extra early in the morning and do your best to be on time, then focus on keeping your timeline running smoothly. Finishing early will always be appreciated by brides, because it will allow more time for their portrait photos before the ceremony.

Occupational Hazards - Protect Your Body
For the longevity of a makeup artist's health, it is vital to have your own portable makeup chair. Endless hours spent working in a bent-over position will dramatically shorten the length of your career.

Hairstylists can often rely on a regular chair that is already in the bridal suite; however, makeup artists will need to bring a tall director's chair or barstool. Your back will thank you!

One telltale sign of a rookie makeup artist is showing up to a job in high heels. We've all done it, myself included. You will kill yourself if you try to work those long hours on your feet in heels. Please don't put yourself at risk of injury just for the sake of looking good. The novelty will wear off very quickly.

Your best bet is a pair of flats with great support or a cute pair of athletic shoes. No one, not even the bride on the most formal day of her life, will look down on you for taking care of yourself.

CHAPTER 18: Bridezillas

Mythical or Real?

Truthfully, whether they're real or a figment of your nightmares depends on your definition of a bridezilla. While the degree of this syndrome varies greatly from bride to bride, a little bit of bridezilla lives inside each and every woman.

Is the anxiety she is experiencing usually directed at her beauty team? For the most part the answer is no. But, it's best to remember this: When she is having that moment … steer clear!

Take a deep breath. Remind yourself that, no matter what's going on right now, the situation is over the second you walk out the door. Focus on exuding a calming energy in the hope that she will be soothed by your Zen attitude and professionalism.

This won't always be possible, but this is just one more reason why no two days on the job are the same and you will likely end up with enough material for your own Lifetime movie.

Reality TV aside, it is really quite normal for a bride to have anxiety on her wedding day. She has been planning the details for more than a year and imagining how this day will play out since she was a little girl.

Today, the families of both the bride and groom are converging to celebrate their marriage, and many of them have never met before. Doesn't that sound stressful to you?

When it comes to delivering client satisfaction, the mothers are typically much more difficult to handle than a nervous bride. I often find that, echoing inside my mind, I hear the saying, "I don't come to your work and tell you how to do your job!" While working with mother of the bride or groom, just do your best work and deliver the highest level of customer service you possibly can.

At the end of the day, it's the bride you need to please, and they are often well aware that their mother is a bit batty. Take their overbearing demands with a grain of salt. If only you were able to personally offer her a glass of champagne.

The bridezillas you need to avoid are the ones who make special demands that go beyond the criteria of your job. If they demand discounts or berate you on the quality or cost of your service, just pass. Brides who display high maintenance behavior before you've even met them should be avoided. Period.

You will not enjoy working with women like these – before or during their wedding day. Even when you are just starting out in your career, avoid these problematic women like the plague.

Never accept difficult clients just to put work on your calendar. They will make you want to run away from weddings as fast as humanly possible. Bridezillas are not worth it. Why let anyone ruin your career for you?

Even the kindest of brides will display *moments* of heightened emotion and anxiety. In the end, they will be so grateful to you when it is all over because you managed to make them feel amazing – all while putting up with crazy moms and getting everyone out the door on time for pictures. Don't be surprised if you receive a kind thank you card or email after she gets back from her honeymoon.

Can you think of a more rewarding feeling than knowing you've helped a woman feel beautiful on her wedding day? She will never forget you for this.

Cherish that feeling and know that, while the beauty industry may seem shallow at first glance, we are given the gift of helping people feel good about themselves, all while earning a respectable livelihood along the way.

SECTION IV:
Marketing Your Talents

CHAPTER 19: Portfolio Building

What Brides Are Looking For

During booking season, when brides are on the hunt for their wedding day beauty team, they scan dozens of portfolios before taking the next step to seek more information from potential artists.

Your portfolio is your company's main visual advertisement and the difference between booking brides and being passed over will depend upon the strength of your online portfolio.

You may spend months, or even years, developing a portfolio that showcases what a well-rounded artist you are. For most makeup artists, their portfolio is a mixed bag of fashion shoots, advertising campaigns, mock weddings and real brides.

Editing your portfolio so that it highlights your artistic abilities can be a challenge no matter your experience level. That's why, just as if you were writing a book, it is worthwhile to consult another trustworthy artist to help you select images that tell the best story about your skill level and the type of work you do as an artist.

In truth, portfolio creation is where many artists fail at the business of makeup artistry. In the long run, including too many repetitive images, showcasing marginal work from your early days or filling your portfolio with the work of amateur photographers will hold you back from booking the clients you deserve.

As a professional artist, it is critical to develop an editorial eye for your work and tell a story about your style through the curated images inside your portfolio. One of a makeup artist's greatest sources of impatience and frustration stems from waiting for photos from past events to arrive.

For instance, you might participate in an amazing wedding with a strikingly beautiful bride. You absolutely cannot wait to add those photos to your portfolio but, after waiting a month or more for the photos, it turns out that the lighting was too dim or the photos catch the bride at weird angles - she flat out doesn't look her best.

Sadly, it happens all too often, we take one look and decide we can't use the images on our website because they don't make for good advertising. The decision not to use these long-awaited, but disappointing, photos is a tough but necessary one.

Potential clients who view sub-par photos in your portfolio will presume this is the level of work you do. It won't matter that you had nothing to do with the photographer's quality of work.

The truth is, brides only want to see photos of other brides you've worked with who look amazing. When choosing images for your portfolio, base your selections on:

The quality of the photography.
How beautiful the bride looks overall.
The quality or detail of your work in the images.

Your bridal portfolio should consist exclusively of brides and past wedding parties. If you work in other fields of professional artistry, keep a separate portfolio or website for that genre of your work.

A well-designed portfolio of beautiful bridal images will keep your story from getting cluttered and perform as a stronger piece of advertising when brides-to-be compare your company with other artists who lump all kinds of portfolio pictures together.

What prospective bridal clients *don't* want to see:

Anything other than bridal work, this includes local fashion shoots you've participated in. This may be repetitive, but this practice is seen in portfolios far too often.

Halloween, special-effects makeup, music videos or film work. *None* of it. They *only* want to see brides. Glittery faces, extra-long lashes, over-zealous theatrical or stripper-inspired makeup should also be avoided. You'd think this would all go without saying, but it's commonplace in too many portfolios.

Avoid boring her with too many images from one wedding. She only wants to see so many angles of each bridal party member.

Before and after photos. Potential bridal clients really don't want to see these. No bride wants to think of herself as a "before." If you do create a phenomenal makeover, feel free to share the images on your blog or Facebook – but they should not be in the main section of your portfolio.

What brides *do* want to see:

A curated series of images that tells a story about your well-rounded professional experience and what you can do to help her feel beautiful on her wedding day.

Ample amounts of professional bridal portraits that are well lit and feature past clients looking drop-dead gorgeous. Make sure to include lots of variety when it comes to styles. Contrary to popular belief, not every bride wants to look "soft and romantic."

A wide diversity of ethnicities and face shapes. This shows that you are highly practiced and comfortable working with just about anyone. Include examples of tattoo cover-up, airbrush foundation and other unique skills you might possess.

Behind-the-scenes photos featuring you working with your brides. These images are worthy of inclusion in your portfolio because behind-the-scenes photos have an inviting quality about them and provide credibility that you are who you say you are.

Camera Phone Shots

If you also style hair for weddings, it's completely acceptable to include camera phone images in your portfolio, as long as they capture the intricate beauty of your bridal hair work. However, makeup artists should steer clear of camera phone shots.

It is very difficult to light a face flatteringly with a camera phone, and these lowbrow photos can actually work against you with potential bride clients.

You're probably wondering, "How do I get my hands on quality photos when I am just starting out?" It's true that, as a novice makeup artist, the hardest images to obtain are those initial professional images you so urgently need for your portfolio.

By following these steps you will be on the path to building a professional quality portfolio that will attract the brides you are after.

Begin by organizing a mock-bridal photo shoot with friends. For this, you will need to be a touch resourceful and get your hands on a used wedding dress. Browse Craigslist or eBay – or even take a trip through a few local thrift stores to see what you can find.

You will also benefit from having a friend who knows a bit about photography and owns a decent camera. Don't know anyone like this? Rent a camera from a local camera shop and do it yourself.

Once you have the dress and photographer lined up, it's time to style one of your friends as if she were a bridal client. It's even better if you can do this with two or three friends to maximize the number of usable images you will get from a single shoot.

You *can* do this with just one wedding dress. Just accessorize it differently for each one of your mock-brides. Don't get too caught up in flawlessness during this photo shoot. These photos don't need to be perfect, they just need to show off your talent and eye for beautiful makeup.

Once you have your mock-bridal images in hand, look up wedding photographers in your area, focusing specifically on photographers who are also just starting out and building their own portfolios. Use search tools on Facebook and Yelp to make a list of budding photographers in your area.

Send each of your potential photographers a short, friendly email letting them know you are a new makeup artist in the area and ask if they would be interested in doing a bridal photo shoot with you. Attach the strongest images from the shoot you did with friends so they can see examples of your work firsthand.

If you can find an interested photographer, great work! Collaborate with them on as many bridal shoots possible. This time, the advantages are two-fold. Not only will the quality of the photography be higher than the shoot you did with friends, you will plant the seed for future bookings as you spread your name around town.

It is possible that you will be able to meet and work with several new photographers this year. Be aware that photographers tend to be very busy with weddings and family portraits during the summer months and also before the holidays. Plan your approach accordingly.

Tip: Make it a personal goal to shoot with one new photographer per month. That way, within six months, you will have the start of a great portfolio to begin showing to interested brides.

How to Get Real Wedding Photos
Once your portfolio is strong enough to help you successfully book weddings, it's time to add photos of actual bride clients. These photos are harder to come by than you might think, because every photographer works differently.
Some will post photos from recent weddings within a few days, while the work of others may not see the light of day for months. Want to learn a trick that will get you photos from almost every wedding you work on?

Tracking brides down after the wedding is no easy task. When brides return from their honeymoons they are busily focused on getting life back to normal following the stress that surrounded their whirlwind wedding experience. If you do send them an email after the honeymoon, make sure your words are thoughtful and gracious, stressing how much you loved being part of their big day.

Kindly ask your bride if she has any photos from the wedding because you would love to feature her in your portfolio. Even if she does respond to your email, she may be able to tell you nothing more than that she doesn't yet have her photos because her photographer will need months to complete them.

A better strategy for getting photos after the wedding begins with the questionnaire contained in your wedding contract. Be sure it includes a line asking for the name of the wedding photographer. Once your bride completes your service agreement, look up the photographer's information and bookmark their website, blog and Facebook account.

Shortly after weddings take place, it is common for photographers to post photos of their recent work because it gives them the opportunity to showcase what they are up to. Plus, newlyweds love to see sneak peaks from their wedding day. The good news for you, as the artist, is that in most cases you can pull these photos for use in your own promotions.

If you do obtain portfolio images via social media, be sure you always give credit where credit is due. When posting these shots to your own social media pages, it is important to link directly to the photographer's Facebook page or website.

Remember, only the photographer owns the copyright, and it is a privilege to be permitted to use these photos to promote your work. Photographers will greatly appreciate your recognition and promotion of their imagery with your followers. Remember, reciprocity goes a long way in this business.

CHAPTER 20: Branding Your Business

When you think about branding, what's the first thing that comes to mind? Most likely, you're picturing the logos of big corporate brands. These companies have teams of marketers whose sole mission is to devise ways to represent the company in a way that not only grabs the attention of their target consumers, but also stays in their mind when it's time to make a purchase.

Similarly, how you choose to brand your wedding artistry business will have a direct effect on the long-term profitability of your company. Just like any small business or large corporation, your brand serves as your company's identity; meaning it is the way you want to be perceived by brides – and by the world.

As the owner of a successful beauty business, you should be able to describe your company using just a few well-chosen words that tell the world who you are and what you do.

Start by making a list of adjectives that you feel symbolize the heart of what you do for a living. Study the logos and slogans of successful businesses (in other fields) that you admire and evaluate the ones that represent the company well. Use this inspiration to begin crafting the name and tag line for your beauty company.

Focus On Your Target Market
Now that you've begun to define your company, take time to focus in on your target bride. Are you after high-end luxury brides? Do you prefer working with median-range spenders or are you aiming for the budget bride? Imagine your preferred client and define who she is on paper.

While you're doing this exercise, have fun playing with the details. How old is she? How much money she is spending on her wedding? Where does she shop? What are her interests, beauty style, etc.?

Identifying your ideal client will help you fine-tune the branding for your business.

How to Choose A Business Name

To avoid pulling your hair out, try to spend no longer than a week dreaming up your business name, or you may never feel like you've found the "perfect name."

There are an endless number of directions you can go with your business name, just make sure to choose something unique and catchy that expresses who you are.

Feeling lost? Using your own name works well for the wedding industry. It sounds professional and will save you from having to register a fictitious business name with your county clerk.

If you do decide to use a fictitious business name, please do yourself a favor by following a few guidelines. Your business name should be easy to understand, reflect who you are and ultimately draw desirable clients your way.

Factors to Consider

You may not have given much thought to the effect of the "Google factor" on your decision as you dream up a name for your company, but you should be factoring in the name's SEO. What exactly does this refer to?

SEO stands for "Search Engine Optimization," and you must take the uniqueness of your name into consideration, as well as how well it will place in Google search rankings.

Look into this through a Google search on the name you are potentially interested in using. If you find that the name is commonly used by similar companies, it may be difficult for you to stand out in the vastness of the internet. On the other hand, if you feel confident that the search volume is low enough, forge right ahead.

Also, be conscious of international trademark laws and make sure the business name you want to use isn't already trademarked by someone else.

Feeling Stuck?

You may get to the point where nothing seems new anymore, but don't despair. Many options are available to help you dream up an original name for your company.

Study wedding blogs to get a sense of the latest trends and combine common words in new ways. The most important thing is to make sure *you* love the name. After all, you will be the one using it every day, singing its praises to the world as you promote your business.

Please! If you gain nothing else from this book, stay completely away from generic beauty terms. Tired, overused branding will not single you out as the leading artist in your area. What does this request refer to? These clichés include, but are not limited to: glitz, glam, sparkle, glitter, and many other tired terms.

Above all else, be you! Be your unique self and you'll find yourself working with exactly the brides who best fit your personality and artistic style.

CHAPTER 21: Pricing Your Services

What if I told you that having the prettiest website paired with a killer portfolio might not be enough to get you the job if your pricing is too low? Or, what if you find that brides are scoffing at your high prices even though they've done their preview session and they are amazed by how beautiful you've made them feel?

Establishing your price list is an art form, one that will take time to perfect. There is a fine line between being priced too low or too high. That's why many large companies hire pricing gurus to hit upon the perfect niche.

Examine how much your target bride has set aside for her bridal beauty budget. Based on your findings, consider how many weddings will be required to bring in enough money to allow you to live the lifestyle you want while saving for the future.

Pricing your services appropriately is very much about perceived value, and it is an essential element of your overall marketing plan. If you are targeting luxury brides, you can't charge what the salon down the street is charging, you need to distinguish your talents as the best in your city.

If mid-tier brides are your focus, you want to be in line with the upper level of what they can spend. That way, they can afford you but still perceive your services as a high-end splurge.

Deciding how to price your services is an art form, and marketing people could spend weeks mulling over the possibilities.

Size Up the Competition
An important factor in pricing your services is evaluating your close competitors' rates. Don't you think McDonalds and Burger King are in constant price wars when they go after the same target customer?

It may seem unreasonable to compare fast food to your high-end bridal company; however, these competitors are a tried-and-true example of using pricing to beat out the opponent and win the targeted customer.

Begin by seeking out at least three beauty companies in your area that you believe target the same type of bride client you are after. It might feel intimidating to contact competitors directly to ask for their pricing sheet. After all, why would they be interested in helping you? You are after a piece of their pie.

Do some sleuthing by discreetly sending an inquiry posing as a new bride interested in their services. They will follow up with a price list and you never have to contact them again.

It may not give you the best feeling to have to contact your competitors this way, but in a world where businesses don't list their pricing on their websites, there is no better way to find out first-hand.

What's Next?
Okay. Now you have an idea of what your competitors are charging. It's time to find the sweet spot that will price your services just high enough to accommodate the lower-end of your market while also attracting the high-end brides you seek to work with.

When you are first starting, it's smart to price yourself in the middle of the pack. Charge enough to make a living, but realize that it will take a few years for you to command the prices you ultimately deserve.

Like any service-oriented business, you must invest the time required to build your reputation. Down the road you will be busy enough to charge more for the quality of your services and ultimate professionalism.

When your calendar is booked solid and you are receiving more wedding requests than you could possibly fulfill, you will know it's time to raise your prices. Until then, stay diligently focused on the growth of your company and know that your time will come.

Always Get Paid Before the Wedding
In a business where you often meet your bride client on the day of her wedding, it would seem that the simplest payment method would be to collect cash at the time of service. Can you believe that, even with the most ironclad wedding contract, it is still possible to get stiffed for payment on the wedding day?

By now, you know that just about anything that *can* go wrong at a wedding *will* go wrong at some point in your career. One of the most common issues is caused by a bridal party member being late for her beauty time slot or missing her session altogether.

Although none of this is your fault, the tension created by requesting payment for the missed service can be completely avoided by requiring full payment up front.

For example, a talented makeup artist was in the middle of a wedding job when the bride got a call from one of her bridesmaids stating that she would not be able to make it for her beauty appointment.

The bridesmaid had forgotten to pack her son's shoes and needed to run off to a store to buy him a pair for the wedding. Even though the artist had done everything right to fulfill her end of the contract, she was not paid for her time or service.

The makeup artist gently mentioned to the bride that payment for her services would still be required per the terms of the contact, but the bride stated that she was so tight on money and couldn't pay for her shoe-shopping friend.

The artist could have pressed the issue, but that would have made things uncomfortable between the bride and herself, and potentially put her in a position to receive a negative review, even though she had done nothing wrong.

To completely avoid situations like this, always require payment two or three weeks before the day of the wedding. This will eliminate unnecessary stress and enable you to offer superior customer service by suggesting that the bride choose someone to take the place of a missing bridesmaid. Win-win for everyone!

Collect Payment In Advance, In One Lump Sum
Beyond requiring payment in advance, it is also advisable to require payment in one lump sum. When first hearing of this policy, some brides will complain that they aren't paying for their bridal party's beauty services and are uncomfortable being responsible for the total balance up front.

Simply state that this is company policy and recommend that she have all of her bridesmaids send payment to her in advance of the wedding. Then she can pool their funds and pay you.

Establishing this policy will save you a lot of trouble in the future. You are an artist, not an accountant, and you do not have time to check off which bridesmaids have sent you payment and which have not. Remember, this is a business and our foremost concern is maximizing your profits.

To make things even easier for you and your clients, consider offering online payment. There are several ways to collect payments online and, although they charge fees, it's better take small fees over the loss of payment for contracted beauty services by those who fail to show up on the day of the wedding.

Payment options worth looking into:
PayPal
World Pay
Intuit Payment Network
Square

CHAPTER 22: Marketing Materials

Now that you have your chosen business name selected, the next step would be to develop your marketing materials. These are the visual elements of your branding you'll use to professionally represent your company to potential brides and make wedding industry connections.

These visual elements of your branding are very important. Done right, they have the power to elevate you above your competition and boost sales.

Logo
It may sound like a no-brainer, but every business needs to have a logo. Even if it is nothing more than your company name written in a simple, classic font. If you are skilled with graphic design, you can do this yourself, but most people would be better served by leaving the job to professionals.

Etsy
www.etsy.com
An incredible source for graphic designers at very affordable prices. Search for logo designs and you will find dozens of beautifully crafted logos, all well within your budget.

Simply make your purchase and send the designer your company's name. In little to no time you will receive your logo in your inbox featuring your chosen design.

The best part of this approach is that many graphic designers on Etsy retire designs after they have been purchased a certain number of times, so you needn't worry about using a generic design that can be seen plastered all over the internet.

Your logo should appear on your website, at the top of your contract and wedding questionnaire, invoices and social media websites. You want brides who are searching for local beauty companies to see your logo in several places around the web and learn to instantly recognize it as yours.

Business Card

With your completed logo, you're ready to create a business card and the other marketing materials you will hand over to brides as you convince them that you are *the* professional artist they should hire. These items can be affordably in a virtually endless number of places.

Check with your Etsy designer. They may be able to print business cards for you. Otherwise, the following sources are suitable for online printing of gorgeous, affordable business cards:

www.moo.com
A wide selection, including mini-cards. Not the cheapest option, but these cards are impactful and less likely to be thrown away.

www.tinyprints.com
Another site with beautiful print options.

www.vistaprint.com
Not the most visually stunning, but a great place to start out if you are on an ultra-tight budget.

When designing your business card, be sure to include your logo, contact information and website address. It's wise to avoid using a photo from your portfolio on your business card. As soon as you print those cards, you will have a new photo that you prefer and wish was on your cards instead.

The true purpose of a business card is to pique the interest of a potential bride client and make her want to visit your website to learn more. Keep things simple – your logo and contact information are all that are required to win her attention.

CHAPTER 23: Building a Powerful Website

The website for your beauty business is the single most important aspect of your marketing program, and this section could easily provide enough content for its own book. The quality of your online presence is likely to make or break your business, but please don't panic.

There is a straightforward way to build a high-quality website that will impress potential brides and boost the number of weddings you book *this* year.

It is so tragic to glimpse some of the poor quality websites makeup artists are using in today's world of modern technology. These artists are seemingly unaware that they are repelling bride clients toward competing artists with a stronger online presence.

A professionally designed website with well-written content and a beautifully edited portfolio will be the deciding factor in influencing brides to choose you above the competition.

This sage advice cannot be stressed enough. Your website is *every*thing. Today's brides are millennials who have been raised on technology. They don't order a pizza anymore without first checking out the restaurant's website and online reviews.

When they're preparing to hire their wedding vendors, you'd better believe they will be vetting you based on the professional quality of your website and sparkling online reviews.

At the heart of it, your website should have a clean design, load quickly and tell a story about your company in the first three seconds after a bride lands on your homepage. What makes the first three seconds so critical? As brides carry out online searches, they may look at the websites of ten or more artists in your area.

If you want to compel brides to spend time getting to you know via your website, it had better load quickly and catch their eye within the first few seconds. If not – they will already be moving on.

Your website does not need a novel's worth of blog posts or a large portfolio. While you should plan to grow your online presence over time, start with just these sections:

Main Page
The landing page should showcase a beautiful photo of your bridal work and a description of what your company does. Don't leave room for any confusion as to what you do or the region where you work. That's it. Nothing more. Keep it clean and simple.

About Your Company
This page tells brides a little more about your company by sharing details about your background. Use this page to tell a story about who you are as an artist and what you love about your career.

Portfolio Gallery
The portfolio section is made up of images you have worked very hard to build. Make sure it is edited so that it tells a story, not only of your artistry, but also how happy and beautiful the brides who work with you are.

Services
List all of the services you offer. Don't expect brides to know exactly what you do or all that you have to offer them. Clearly informing them on what you have to offer will save you time in answering the same questions over and over via email.

Social Media Links
Share links to each of your social media platforms, giving brides the opportunity to dive in even deeper as they get to know you. Keep brides browsing longer by sharing imagery via social media that won't be on your business website.

Blog

If you have a blog, a direct link should be front and center on your website. Blogging offers you an opportunity to share your voice with your audience and give your perspective on past weddings you've been part of. Even if you don't enjoy writing, there are many benefits to blogging.

Contact Page

When listing your contact information, make it easy for brides to get in touch with you to inquire about your availability and pricing for their wedding date. It's preferable to use websites that offer a contact form you can create yourself. This will help direct questions from brides and let you gather information needed to give inquiring brides a proper sales quote.

The contact form should ask for:

- The bride's name
- An email address
- Phone number
- Wedding date
- Wedding venue
- Number in the wedding party
- Comments

By having all of that information ahead of time, you will be in a position to respond with a much stronger sales pitch than if all you have to go on is an email address with vague questions about your pricing.

Writing Content for Sales

To put your best foot forward when it comes to grabbing the attention of newly engaged women, the wording of your website should be carefully crafted to persuade brides to reach out to learn more about what your services can do for them. Finish strong on each page with a "call to action" that says something like:

"Contact me today for a quote!"

"Now booking weddings for the upcoming season!"
"Inquire today for availability and pricing!"

Sound cheesy? Part of becoming a well-rounded business owner is gaining an understanding of sales techniques. Your website is the paramount opportunity to get brides to hire you. Why not put every effort into being the one they choose?

Should You List Your Pricing on Your Website?

Opinions on this topic vary. My personal feeling is that your website should *not* list your prices. Its purpose is to create an engaging platform that piques a bride's interest and entices her to learn more.

By choosing to send your price list only through a carefully crafted email, you have the chance to share a little of your own personality, and get to know your potential client a bit more through asking specific questions about her wedding plans.

Remember, a new bride will look into several beauty companies before making her selection. When she reaches out to you via email to request information about your services, availability and pricing, it's your opportunity to impress her with your personality and genuine interest in bringing her bridal beauty ideas to life for her.

If you were to list your pricing on your website, the basic message a potential bride perceives is, "Take a look. If my company is in your budget, get in touch."

A superior message to send would be, "I am great at what I do and would love to have the opportunity to style you on your wedding day. I hope you are interested in my talents. Please take a look at the price list and tell me more about your ideas for your wedding day beauty look."

In this highly competitive industry, it's very hard to win clients based on pricing alone, making it a race to the bottom among competing artists. Charge what you are worth and educate brides on why they should hire you.

Building Your Website

Now that you know the subject matter to highlight on your website, it's time to produce this powerful online platform for your company. Can you, with little or no experience, build a website that will sell your artistry skills to brides? Can you do this in just a few hours? Yes, you absolutely can.

Template-based websites enable you to simply plug your information and photos into a website design that a web designer has already created.

Template websites are affordable, and many offer great design features. This type of website will do the work for you – without taking time away from what truly makes you money – your makeup business!

www.creativemotiondesign.com
The top pick for hosted template-based websites offering new artists many design options to choose from that won't break the bank. CMD has great extra features like SEO compatibility, a built in WordPress blog and social media plug-ins. In addition they offer excellent customer service and reliability.

www.bigfolio.com
Another great template-based web host. The prices are a bit higher than those of Creative Motion Design, but BigFolio offers crisp, clean designs that will showcase your work beautifully and impress prospective bride clients.

Avoid Common Mistakes

Looking for a sure-fire way to repel brides and blend in with the pack? Building your own website when you do not have a background in web design is guaranteed to make you look like an amateur artist. Your website is your *number one* advertising tool and, for that reason, it is imperative that you put your best foot forward.

Put the needs of your company first. Don't waste your time attempting to design your own website through Wix, WordPress or any other "free" website offer.

None of these freebie companies will elevate the professionalism of your business above the competition or attract the bride clients you want to work with.

Domain Names
Your website address should be comprised of your business name such as www.bloomingartistry.com and not a free sub-website such as bloomingartistry.wix.com or bloomingartistry.wordpress.com.

Purchasing the domain name of your company will cost approximately $12. For the same price as a tube of mascara you will own the web presence for your artistry business.

In most cases you can purchase your domain name through the template-based web host of your choosing. Otherwise, www.godaddy.com allows you to purchase domain names at affordable rates.

One last piece of advice when it comes to exhibiting your prowess online – avoid music on your website. Brides often do their wedding planning during the workday and do not need to get busted by their boss for not being focused on work when your song starts blasting in the office. Additionally, you should not expect clients to appreciate your musical taste. Sorry.

CHAPTER 24: Blogging

Do you know the one simple step you can take on a weekly basis to boost your web traffic, show off your artistic abilities and point out what makes you better than the competition? All while sharing your personality with interested brides without ever getting them on the phone?

Believe it or not, blogging has the capability to do all of these things if you are willing to sit down at your computer just once a week.

Blogging grants brides a chance to dive further into your work and get to know you a bit more through the way you describe your artistry and passion for your clients. To keep the process simple, most template-based websites offer you a WordPress-based blog that's built right into the interface of your website.

In addition to building a stronger connection with your target client, there are also unseen benefits to your overall marketing plan. These days, Google search rankings are based on the quality of content contained within a website. Meaning, the more often your website is updated with fresh content, the higher you will rise in Google search results.

Techniques for staying ahead of your competition change often, read up on the latest SEO (search engine optimization) practices, either online or by purchasing an e-book from Amazon that was written this year as anything older may contain outdated information.

Consistency Is Key
If putting your thoughts in writing is a new experience for you, sharing your voice can be a real test in the early stages of blogging. As a business owner who wears all the hats, scheduling time to sit down and write can be easily forgotten when tending to other aspects of the business.

Building a blogging schedule into your monthly calendar will help keep you on track for posting consistently. If parking yourself once a week to write a blog post isn't realistic or enjoyable for you, sit down just two times a month to write two blog posts each time. Post one immediately and schedule the other to go live the following week.

Pushing your writing time out any further could easily slip into the realm of procrastination. It may require great effort to take a seat and write blog posts once a month, increasing the likelihood that you will forget to do it altogether.

Developing a regular blogging habit will not only boost your web traffic, it will also clue brides in to just how busy you are. Hint: they should be working with you too!

Fresh Blogging Ideas
Just what are you going to say to your target bride client? Topics are endless and your posts are limited only by your creativity. Below are a few ideas that will have you continually publishing fresh content:

- Real weddings you've participated in
- Styled shoots you've worked on for wedding blogs
- Beauty tips
- Hair and makeup tutorials
- Client before-and-afters
- Beauty product reviews
- Team bios
- Stories on other wedding vendors you love working with

You may find that other wedding vendors are sharing your blog posts on their social media platforms if they also participated in a real wedding you've blogged about. This is an excellent way to be seen by potential new brides who have hired their coordinator, photographer or florist, but haven't yet booked their beauty team.

The more you promote others, the likelier they are to promote you. Always be sure you credit the photographer if you use real wedding photos. They own the copyright on their photos and will greatly appreciate that you've thoughtfully endorsed their business.

CHAPTER 25: Social Media

How can you connect with your clients and attract newly engaged women without ever spending a dime on advertising? Beyond the power of expanding your web presence and visibility, harnessing the power of social media can help book weddings for you in just ten minutes per day. Let's face it, you're spending endless hours on social media as it is, why not utilize this time to grow your business?

Begin by opening social media accounts in your company's name. These pages should be separate from your personal accounts and should focus only on your work or posting content you are excited about that is related to the beauty or wedding industry. Share often and make sure to post things your target audience will enjoy.

The better your content, the more engaging you will be with your followers – and more likely to attract new ones. Around the world, couples get engaged every day, and the size of the audience you can build is limited only by how motivated you are with social media.

How to Build an Audience
When you are just starting out, building a solid number of followers from scratch may seem like a daunting challenge. Inviting your friends and family to follow your business is a noble way to get started.

Share links to your company's social media platforms with everyone you know and ask them to share with their friends. You may be surprised at who is willing to help you along the way.

Giveaways
A giveaway contest offering a little something brides would covet is a great way to grow your following. Something along the lines of a makeup goody bag filled with your favorite products would be very well received.

Plan to spend some money putting the gift bag together, but the costs will be far outweighed by the benefits the contest garners in the form of new followers.

Example:
Hold a contest on Facebook stating that you are planning a fun, exciting makeup giveaway. State that, once your page reaches a specific number of likes, you will choose a winner from among your followers. To enter the contest, all your followers have to do is share your Facebook page with their friends.

You may decide to choose a winner by keeping a list of the people who shared your page or simply choose one of your followers at random. Women love opportunities to win contests, so your web traffic should receive a healthy boost. Besides, it's fun to get your base excited about what you do!

Time Saving Tips
Worried that you don't have the time, or enough content to be shared over multiple social networks? Optimize the time you spend by telling different variations of the same story through each of your accounts.

For example, once you have the photos back from a real wedding you worked on, write a blog post detailing your reflections on the day, your experience working with the bride, her inspirations for the look she chose along with techniques you used to create the look.

Give credit where it is due. Cross-promote other wedding vendors who were involved in the same wedding by tagging their accounts in your blog post. Your story will appear in front of their audience just as you have promoted their company to your own followers.

Below are some tips for maximizing the potential of one blog story over each social network:

Facebook
Post a link to the blog post you've penned about a recent wedding using your favorite photo from the day in the post. Tag every vendor that you know worked on the wedding, including the photographer, coordinator, florist, cake company, the venue itself, etc. (This is why

it is important to pay attention to every vendor who participates in the weddings you work on!).

Instagram
Post a different photo from the same wedding and emphasize how beautiful the bride looks, tagging any vendors you worked with. Remember to use relevant hash tags to attract an even larger audience.

Pinterest
Select a detailed photo of the bride that shows off your artistic abilities, then link back to your blog post and explain how you did it. Good examples of this would be a close up of the eyes, hairstyle or any other beautiful detail you fashioned for the bride or her bridesmaids.

Twitter
Share an interesting, relevant fact about the wedding that might intrigue potential clients or other wedding vendors to click through to your blog post. Don't forget to also include related hash tags.

A thought on hash tags. It's best to draw on only a few per post, overuse of hash tags will appear overly promotional and self-serving. Focus on sharing things you are excited about and your followers will take notice of your enthusiasm.

Relevant Wedding Hash Tags:
#weddingbeauty
#weddinghair
#weddingmakeup
#sayyestothedress
#bridalbeauty
#bridalmakeup
#bridalhair
#thenameofthevenue
#yourcompanyname
#weddingideas
#weddinginspiration
#weddingbells

#weddingphoto
#weddingstyle
#bridalparty
#bridalstyle
#makeupartist
#updo
#weddingstylist
#bridalhairstylist
#bridalhairstyle

The Most Powerful Social Network of All

Would you believe me if I told you that one social network alone could catapult your business to success and help book weddings soon after you establish your web presence – all for free? I know. It sounds almost too good to be true. But the powerful effect that Yelp can have on your business is well worth the time investment on your part.

Yelp has succeeded in becoming the modern-day Yellow Pages. When searching for a business online, the company's Yelp page often comes up in the number one position, even before the company's own website.

Yelp has built a powerful network based on user reviews and brides look to Yelp everyday, checking for feedback about others' experiences with wedding professionals.

Does it sound peculiar that the same website people visit to look up a local dry cleaner is also the one they use to search for wedding vendors? At first, I was skeptical too – and slow to jump on the Yelp train.

Unexpectedly, Yelp is a powerful search tool that brides are actively utilizing to learn about potential wedding vendors. The best part is that it costs you nothing to create a page for your business!

Below are a few suggestions to help you leverage the power of Yelp for your makeup artistry business:

After taking the initial steps to create your Yelp page, indulge in as much detail as possible when filling out your business information. Include lots of photos, a powerful description of your business and a link to your website.

Your goal is to create such a level of interest in what they see on Yelp that brides immediately click through to your website to learn more about what you do.

Keep in mind, the most important aspect of your Yelp page is user reviews. Do your best to get past clients to review your services on Yelp. Yelp is very vocal about the types of reviews they prefer on the site and frown upon business owners asking people to write reviews on behalf of their business.

Regardless, do your best to reach out to past clients and ask them to write a review of their experiences with your company. It's just a fact that the more reviews your company has, the more traffic your Yelp page will receive. Translation? More brides will want to book you.

Negative Reviews
While these words may be easier said than done, *please* don't panic if someone writes a sour review about their encounter with you or your company. It happens to everyone at some point, as the work we do is a subjective art, there is no way you can possibly please everyone.

The best thing you can do to avoid negative feedback online is to always be professional and give your clients an amazing customer service experience. Even if they weren't the biggest fan of the makeup look you created for them, brides are unlikely to write a negative review online if they enjoyed your personality and service.

Typically, the ones who pen negative reviews online you won't see coming. This is because the time you spent with them will not have been remembered as particularly negative or dramatic from your perspective. Some women write terrible things about almost all of their vendors.

If you scan through all of the reviews this person has written, you will often notice the pattern of an overwhelmingly negative person with impossible expectations. Unfortunately, it is unattainable to satisfy certain people and not one more moment of your thoughts should be wasted on these women. Just stay focused on receiving positive reviews from happy clients.

Fact: Having a couple of bad reviews among many upbeat reviews actually increases your credibility with potential brides scanning your Yelp page. If all of your reviewers gave you 5-stars, brides would be secretly questioning the trustworthiness of your Yelp reviews.

Paid Advertising with Yelp
As far as opportunities for your business with Yelp ads, the options are plentiful. If the pricing fits your marketing budget; they may be worth a trial period during the peak-booking season.

What to Say to Get a Bride to Write You a Review
It can be extremely intimidating to reach out to a past client after the wedding to encourage her to write a review on behalf of your business. Oftentimes, brides can be so emotional on their wedding day that, in the back of your mind, you are not even confident that they were happy with your services.

In most cases, the truth is that they loved having you as part of their big day and would be happy to spend a few minutes writing a helpful review for your business.

About a month after the wedding, send your bride a kind email thanking her for choosing you as one of her trusted vendors for her wedding day. Share something personal about the experience and be genuine.

Mention that, if it isn't too much trouble, it would mean so much if she could take five minutes to write a review about her experience with your company and mention that it would assist future brides in making decisions about who to hire and help your business grow.

Include a direct link to the website where you want her to write a review, do this to make it as easy as possible for her. The harder or more time consuming the process, the less likely she is to write a review of your services.

If you don't hear back, try to reach out through a different medium. Both The Knot and Wedding Wire have review collector tools that will send emails to your brides asking for reviews on your behalf.

The request won't come directly from your email address, so it won't seem as if you are nagging at them repeatedly. Making the most of these tools is great strategy for keeping your business on their minds!

If you've asked twice without success, it's best to step back and move on. The bride is probably too busy and you are wasting valuable time that can be focused on reaching new clients. There will always be more brides and, eventually, you will have dozens of positive reviews.

CHAPTER 26: Paid Advertising

Congratulations! By now, your business has reached new milestones, brides are buzzing and the money is starting to roll in. It's time to take the next step of adding paid advertising to your marketing plan.

When done right, these promotions can actually double your business. Capitalize on the power of advertising by having your branding in the right places at the right times when brides are looking to hire.

The instant as your website goes live, expect to receive dozens of advertising offers from solicitors. Equal parts exciting and nerve-racking, be aware that all your advertising programs should begin with a trial period only. Keep successful programs going strong and if a promotion isn't working for you, cut your losses and try something new.

When deciding between different forms of paid advertising, don't be immediately put off by the price tag. *Remember*, your most expensive advertising is not the one with the highest monthly fee but the one that does the least for you. Meaning, a $200 per month ad that brings you $1,000 per month in business is less expensive than an ad that costs $100 per month and brings in $300 per month.

There are seemingly limitless ways to reach brides through advertising promotions in the world of modern media. From local bridal magazines to online directories, don't be alarmed if you are contacted weekly by sales reps pitching you their latest deals.

While the quality of advertising options and resulting traffic to your website may vary from city to city, online vendor directories are a powerful way to reach brides. Unlike print media, online listings allow you to capture the attention of potential clients at the very moment they are searching for vendors.

Top Picks
www.theknot.com

The Knot is an amazing resource and, at some point, you should strongly consider advertising with this company. Eight out of ten new brides do their wedding planning on The Knot. While The Knot commands high prices for their ad space, it just makes sense to be where the brides are.

If you do decide to advertise on The Knot, make sure to collect reviews from your brides on their sister site www.weddingchannel.com. An annual contest is held in each city to choose The Knot's "Best of Weddings" award. Winning this contest, which is based on reviews from real brides, will boost your presence in their listings even further.

www.weddingwire.com

While smaller than The Knot, this web directory is also used by thousands of active brides. Other benefits include loads of educational resources to help you grow your wedding business, a great review collector tool and a local "Bride's Choice Award" awarded yearly.

International
Both of these companies have international versions of their websites and vendor directories. Conduct an online search of wedding vendor directories in your region. Then, if you see that your biggest competition is advertising in these websites or magazines, it may be worth a trial period on your part.

Facebook
Consider targeting brides in your area through Facebook ads during booking season (the off-season to your local busy season). Make sure to feature high quality images that link directly to your website.

The best part of Facebook ads is the ability to focus on very detailed targeting, they practically hand you your target customer. Facebook ads provide the option to target only women whose marital status is listed as engaged.

Wedding Blogs
Popular wedding blogs, such as Style Me Pretty, Wedding Chicks and Green Wedding Shoes allow a select number of vendors to advertise in their preferred vendor directories.

Bloggers are selective and approval is required, but brides spend significant time on these blogs daily. Being listed as a preferred vendor will boost your web traffic and potentially close the sale based on the stamp of approval received from these coveted blogs.

Print Advertising
In the world of modern media where magazines are a dying channel, it is challenging to speak on the effectiveness of print advertising in bridal magazines. Is there is a direct correlation between brides flipping through a magazine and then going online to visit the website of a bridal beauty company they saw in print?

Truth-be-told, the safer bet is to take out a listing in online bridal directories and put your focus on social media. Most brides do at least some of their wedding planning during their workday and, while it is easy to hide a website you've been browsing from your boss, a magazine is a lot harder to conceal.

Contemplate print magazines only after you are happy with the results from your marketing program and feel ready to add another advertising channel. Don't be afraid to take risks. Most advertising contracts start at six months and one booking can mean you break even on the cost.

Where NOT to Advertise
As a business owner, it is your duty to protect the reputation of your brand. That means it's just as important to know where *not* to be seen, as it is to choose the right places to advertise. Avoid these websites like the plague:

Craigslist
Anyone looking for beauty services on Craigslist is not an ideal client for you. It's fair to say that they have little to no budget and

are only looking for the cheapest of the cheap. Watch out for postings from brides seeking free beauty services for their wedding in exchange for photos for your portfolio.

You already know what it takes to get portfolio photos without being taken advantage of by clients. These types of brides are notoriously difficult to be around. As people who want something for nothing, it is unlikely that they will be satisfied with the beauty look you've created.

Thumbtack
Here, people create posts based on services they are searching for to see who will reply with availability and pricing. Clients who are searching via Thumbtack are bargain hunters, concerned with price more than quality.

Remember, trying to win on price is a race to the bottom. Charge what you are worth and teach brides why they should hire you. This proven strategy will keep you in business for many years.

CHAPTER 27: Bridal Show Pros & Cons

Beyond magazines, wedding blogs and Pinterest, brides are looking for in-person opportunities to see, touch and taste what vendors can do. For many years, bridal shows have been a great opportunity to meet brides face to face and show off what you can do for them via live demos and mini-consultations.

Despite the benefits of face-to-face meetings, with today's millennial brides, the best way to reach them is to be seen online. The quality of bridal expos varies from region to region and show to show.

Some bridal shows very high-end and attract motivated brides looking to book vendors. Others haven't had an update to their format since 2002 and will be nothing more than an exhausting waste of your time and money.

If you do decide to take a leap and sign up for a local bridal show, it's important that you go into it with a strategy to engage brides and entice them to give you their contact information.

To be successful with bridal shows, you must walk out of there with a list of potential brides that you will reach out to after the show is over. Without this list, you just paid a whole heap of money to hand out your business card.

When it comes to how you will represent your company at a bridal show, your booth should be stylish and show off your artistic capabilities in an impressive way. Highlight your brand identity, the services your company offers and why past brides love you so much.

Draw prospective clients in through mini-sessions that show attendees can sign up for. The one-on-one contact will offer you a chance to chat with brides about their ideas and give them a sample of what you can do for their unique style and taste.

Prizes & Giveaways

Unfortunately, it's not enough to simply showcase your company's booth at a bridal expo. To make it worth your while, you need to leave the event with a list of email addresses. One great way to get this list without being overly aggressive is to offer a giveaway that brides can sign up for at the show. This giveaway might be a free preview session, engagement photo makeup, or session before her bachelorette party.

After the show, contact the lucky bride to let her know she's won a session with you. Additionally, you should send an email to all brides from the show reminding them of your company and wedding services.

Sales Incentives

One sage piece of advice to help make the most of a bridal expo is to offer an incentive discount to show attendees. Something along the lines of a 10% discount (or other amount of your choice) off their wedding day beauty services if they book your company before a certain date (two or three weeks out from the show).

Sending brides an email blast that includes a time-sensitive deadline will encourage them to book you sooner rather than later. It's a proven sales strategy that will also help you evaluate the true results from the show and decide whether it is worthwhile to participate in the bridal expo again in the future.

How to Find First-Rate Bridal Shows

New bridal shows seem to be popping up all the time, and it's getting harder to tell which ones are lucrative and which shows should be avoided. Only you can decide if a show is right for your business, and sometimes you just have to take a risk.

When deciding to book a space at a bridal expo, keep in mind the start-up costs of outfitting your booth. Of course you will be able to re-use your design for multiple shows, but it will be costly to decorate your table, have a professional banner made, print out marketing materials for brides to take with them, etc. Choose shows wisely and make sure your target clients will be attending before you incur these expenses.

One way you can judge a show's worthiness is to use your sleuthing skills to examine the list of vendors who participated last year. Most shows feature that list right on their website. Go through the listing and decide if those vendors are of the same caliber as your company.

Your business will be judged by the company you keep, so it's important to be seen among the crowd of vendors that will impress your targeted bride.

If you don't like what you see after reading through the list of last year's vendors, simply pass on the show. Wait until your budget is big enough to exhibit at the high-end bridal expos that offer you the greatest potential for booking brides.

If all of this seems overwhelming, or if it's just too soon for you, begin by simply attending bridal shows in your area as a guest. Walking the floor will give you a feel for the pulse of what's going on in your local wedding community. You'll also have opportunities to introduce yourself to other wedding professionals you've never met before.

Don't be surprised if your visit to the expo inspires ideas for a killer booth that will wow brides when you do want to join in!

CHAPTER 28: Vendor Referrals

Now that you are familiar with the power of social media and paid advertising, it's time to consider new possibilities for attracting bride clients. Booking weddings without having to pay for advertising keeps your overhead expenses low and puts more money in your pocket.

No idea on how to receive bride referrals for free? The truth is that most brides start from scratch when choosing their wedding vendors and don't know where to launch their search. When it comes to making hiring decisions, brides are more likely to go with a recommendation from a trusted source as opposed to browsing options online.

Being part of a local network of wedding professionals can do terrific things to boost business. The more vendors you meet and work with on a regular basis, the more likely you are to collect referrals from brides who need hair and makeup services for their wedding day.

Remember, people refer people they like to work with themselves. It may take time to build relationships with other vendors, but investing your time in building strong partnerships can be very beneficial for your sales.

The most common referrals will come to you via wedding coordinators and photographers, so these vendors are especially important people to get to know. Tread carefully in the early stages of this process.

Be kind and always exude professionalism while in the presence of industry colleagues. It is important that they feel confident in your professionalism and skill if they are to share your name with their brides.

Since the beauty team is often one of the last wedding services the bride books, it can be difficult for us to refer other vendors. When you *do* have an opportunity to offer a referral, however, it will be most appreciated by the reciprocating company!

How to Meet Wedding Professionals

Search online for vendors (i.e., wedding planners, florists, photographers, etc.) in your area whom you believe target your type of bride client. Once your business is up and running, you will want to reach out to these vendors to introduce yourself and let them know you are booking brides for this year's wedding season.

When making contact, display genuine interest in what *they* do for a living. Gain insights into their work by following their social media accounts. Companies who target the same type of client will be the most likely to refer you.

Attend Industry Functions

Even if you won't be exhibiting, it's important to grace bridal shows with your presence for the chance to meet new vendors and catch up with colleagues you haven't seen in a while. By staying on their radar screen, your company will be in the forefront of their minds when a bride asks for a recommendation.

Local professional associations also offer great networking opportunities and will keep you informed about what's going on in your region. Typically, for wedding planners or photographers, some of these groups are open to all areas of the wedding business.

www.thursdaytherapy.net
Visit Thursday Therapy to see if there is a fun networking group in your region. No luck? Consider starting a local chapter, they are looking to add new cities!

Styled Photo Shoots

Vendors often collaborate on mock weddings a.k.a. styled shoots aimed at large audiences. Participating in a styled photo shoot to be published on one of the major wedding blogs is a worthy occasion for building new industry connections and showing off your beauty talents.

Often, when we work with brides, we only get to create the looks they are after. Getting involved in these shoots means having a refreshing opportunity to be creative and showcase your own crave-worthy ideas.

Networking Tips
Simply introducing yourself to a new aquaintance and handing them your business card is the best way to be forgettable. If you want to leave a lasting impression, be engaging. Ask about their work and learn about what they do.

Displaying interest in their business increases the likelihood that they will, in turn, want to know about what you do. Follow up afterwards by connecting through social media and do your best to stay on their radar long after your meeting.

Exemplify Gratitude
No matter how many times a wedding coordinator has sent brides your way, always respond with a kind thank you email or card. These invaluable referrals are never to be taken for granted.

Can you imagine if you sent someone work and they never thanked you? By being gracious, you will ensure that colleagues continue sending brides your way.

The Coveted Preferred Vendor List
Many wedding venues, as well as other wedding professionals such as photographers and wedding coordinators, keep a directory of vendors they enjoy working with – and give the list out to their engaged couples. Inclusion in these lists will bring you major competitive advantages in the form of free advertising.

Taking the necessary steps to be included on the preferred vendor lists of the top wedding venues in your area is of particular value to your bridal makeup company. Since the venue is frequently the first thing booked by newly engaged couples, these couples are often a clean slate when it comes to the other vendors they plan to hire. It is well worth going the extra mile to be the first name brides see when looking for beauty professionals.

Sorry to say, there is no magic formula that guarantees placement in these directories. The process is highly competitive and you may have to be part of weddings at a venue for a couple of years before consideration.

Use your detective skills to learn the name of the venue's on-site wedding coordinator and do your best to get your artistry seen by the person in this vital position.

To make the process easy, include a line in your wedding contract asking brides for the name of their on-site wedding coordinator. Then make an effort to introduce yourself to that person while you are at the venue on the date of the wedding.

After the big day, send a brief email to re-introduce yourself. Let the coordinator know how much you enjoyed working at their venue and that you would love to be considered for the beauty category of their preferred vendor list.

If you have tracked down the photos from the wedding you participated in, it's a great idea to include a few in your email so the coordinator can witness first-hand what a great job you've done working with their bride. If the bride has left you an online review, it's an even better idea to share a link to that review with the venue's on-site wedding coordinator.

There is no sure-fire way to make this happen for your company. Just remain consistent with the follow-up. Accept the fact that you could write the most beautifully crafted email, and receive nothing more than a reply stating they aren't considering new additions to their vendor list until next year.

Be tenacious – find out when they will be revising the list and follow up during that time. Polite persistence is the key to eventual inclusion on the preferred vendor directory.

CHAPTER 29: Top Sales Techniques for Booking More Brides

Now that you have a great marketing plan and first-hand knowledge of what it takes to work with brides, your email inbox should start to fill up with inquiries from newly engaged brides seeking to book their wedding day beauty teams.

A bride is often sending quote requests out to several companies, and she will make her decision based on the responses she gets. Your reply to her initial request is critical in closing the sale and beating out the competition.

Hopefully, you have chosen a website template that requires a prospective bride to fill out a contact form with the details of her wedding when emailing to inquire about your pricing and availability. You can take that information and respond in a way that will help you make the sale in the event that she is the right client for you.

Avoid blending in with the crowd by shunning the use of cookie-cutter email responses that list *only* your pricing and availability. Above all, be professional and engaging. Show genuine interest in working with her. The fastest way to lose a bride's attention after she receives your price sheet is to send a generic, impersonal reply.

This woman has already looked over your entire website and is intrigued enough to inquire about your pricing. Now, she wants to know more about your services and get an impression of your personality. Mention how much you love her chosen venue and tell her you'd love to hear about her beauty ideas right from the initial point of contact.

To build on winning sales techniques, start a conversation with her and really listen to what she has to say, whether it is via email or over the phone.

The best salespeople are not those who go on and on with their sales pitch. Instead, it's the ones who listen to the client's needs and then explain how they are the perfect one to deliver exactly that.

The more questions you ask, the more comfortable brides will be with you, and the more likely she will be to hire your company for her wedding day. It really *is* that simple.

The Competitive Edge
I can't tell you how many times I have been told by brides and other wedding professionals how glad they are to have found my company – because no other artists they contacted bothered to respond to them. Hair and makeup professionals are notoriously flakey and do not instill confidence in regards to reliability.

By responding to every email inquiry you receive within 24 hours, you prove yourself to be better than the competition based on your professionalism and quality customer service. Pair that with your stellar artistry skills and you are destined for success.

Going on vacation or know you can't respond within 24 hours? Put your inbox on an "out of office" auto-responder that lets people know when you will be back to work and responding to their email.

Include a Call To Action
Another helpful tip that can help get brides interested in working with you is to be sure your initial response email includes a call to action.

It can be as simple as "I would love to hear more about your hair and makeup ideas for your wedding day. We are now booking preview sessions for this coming wedding season – book before (this day) and receive complimentary airbrush foundation!"

Offering a small incentive will pique her interest and give her a reason to take the next step toward hiring you. Brides have so much going on and endless decisions to make, encouraging her to take action will put you a step ahead of the competition.

Discounts – Bad for The Bottom Line

Only you can decide what pricing plan is right for the profitability of your company; it's wise to limit pricing discounts to bridal shows or during times that a discount will serve as a powerful motivator... A small incentive similar to the one above will sweeten the deal for brides, but that is where the line should be drawn.

In the long run, people who nag you for a discount end up being the worst clients. They expect more for less and will work you to the bone. Set yourself up for financial success by positioning your services competitively. Offer value to the client, but command the rates you deserve. Never let anyone talk you out of what you are worth.

You are one of the few brave souls who has taken a leap of faith and forged ahead on an unknown path in order to follow your dreams. Protect not only your bottom line but also your love for your career by choosing to work only with those who respect and value what you do.

SECTION V:
BOOSTING PROFITS

CHAPTER 30: Managing Your Earnings

In the early stages of your career, any money coming in at all makes you feel like you've won a jump-for-joy victory. Quelling the temptation to buy new clothes and makeup for your kit can be extremely difficult to overcome. During my first taste of success, I found myself wandering into Sephora with a pounding heart, feeling like an alcoholic in a liquor store.

At this point, your calendar is filling up for this year's wedding season and everything is going well. When your phone is ringing off the hook it seems impossible to imagine that the upcoming slow season won't pass you by altogether.

Even for artists at the top of their game, business will always present ups and downs – and you need to be financially prepared. If you plan to stay in business more than a couple of years, it's vital to manage your business so that you have lasting job security, something very hard for freelancers to come by.

For instance, are you saving thirty percent of your income for taxes? How about saving your profits from the busy season to help pay the bills during the off-season?

Even in places like California and Hawaii, where people travel to get married in the warm weather, local makeup artists experience seasonal business fluctuations. Sadly, your landlord is unlikely to accept free makeup sessions as payment during the slow season.

Those pesky bills and taxes can pile up quickly if your funds aren't divided up into the proper savings accounts from the get-go. What about saving to buy a house, or for your retirement? You don't have an employer setting up these accounts on your behalf, so it's your responsibility to build your own future.

Taking these steps from the beginning vastly increases your chances of avoiding burnout and enjoying a long-lasting career in the beauty industry.

As well as hiring a tax accountant, consult your local banker to discuss the best options for retirement savings and investment accounts. When you are young, I know how hard it is to imagine that your circumstances may change or that you will want to spend less time working long hours on your feet down the road.

Ten years from now, however, you will be eternally grateful that you were so diligent in planning for and creating future wealth and happiness.

CHAPTER 31: Examining Income & Expenses

While it's easy to learn about the fun aspects of the business such as new trends and product releases, the purpose of this book is to make you into the most business-savvy makeup artist you can be. An important part of being in business is keeping track of the flow of what's coming in and what's going back out as expenses.

You can make this aspect of the business as streamlined as possible on yourself by using simple accounting software to track all of your income and expenses as you go. By plugging in all of the numbers on a regular basis, you'll find that your software will build reports and give you insights into your business, as well as make sure you're prepared come tax season.

Sit down once a week on a pre-determined day to log all income and expenses into your accounting software. Staying on top of this will take you fifteen minutes, and will be well worth the commitment. If you decide to do it once a month, you risk losing receipts and forgetting certain expenses – and these can mount up over time, costing you money.

Spare yourself from becoming a hair-pulling-stress-ball by tracking your finances weekly. You'll soon learn that the less painful the experience is for you, the better your accounting skills will become.

GoDaddy Bookkeeping
Formerly known as Outright, this free accounting program is the one I have used with my business for years. There is an option to upgrade to a premium account that offers valuable reports and tax information.

QuickBooks
Considered the best small business account program on the market right now, QuickBooks has the most streamlined interface and their

variety of detailed reports is a major bonus. QuickBooks is not a free service, but the monthly fee is worth it if your business grows to a point where you need to progress beyond what GoDaddy offers. It also integrates seamlessly with Intuit Payment Network if you will be collecting payment this way.

Things You Will Be Tracking
Income – payments from preview sessions, deposits received to hold wedding dates, wedding day services and any other forms of income you receive.

Expenses – makeup supplies, meals while working, advertising costs, office supplies, mileage you drive to wedding jobs, etc. Check with your tax accountant for a list of items you will be able to write off on your tax return.

Dive Into Your Reports
To make the most of your accounting software, take the time to analyze your income and expense reports. How much are you bringing in during your busiest months, and just how long is your slow season? What expense category are you spending the most on, and where can you trim the fat?

Owning this knowledge and adapting your goals based on your findings will help ensure your long-term success.

CHAPTER 32: Reining In Product Costs

All seriousness aside, during my first couple of years as an artist, I wanted to own all the makeup in the world. My rationale? A good makeup artist is always ready to work with any face on the planet, so I could never be *too* prepared. Meaning, I couldn't have too much makeup.

Oddly enough, this turned out to be untrue. Since then, I have given a lot of product away to my team members and friends, but I still have makeup I don't think I'll ever use. The importance for you, as a new artist, to make the right choices when building and re-stocking your makeup kit can't be stressed enough.

One very important thing I've learned from my mistakes is to ask myself this question when I am considering making a makeup purchase: "Do I *really* need this product to do my job?"

If the answer is no, I have to consider whether I'm willing to do extra work to make up for the lost profits this purchase will cause? That answer, too, is often no. As you can imagine, my makeup kit has shrunk over the years. Now, when I do make purchases, these are the products I look for.

Pre-Made Palettes

Most major brands put out palettes loaded with an array of eye shadow colors, and some even include blush and bronzer. The sizes of the shadows are a bit smaller than individually packaged ones, but it is so rare to completely use up an eye shadow that you really don't save much by buying the larger sizes.

These pre-packaged palettes give you a major price break, and the makeup brands often combine beautiful colors that help you do your job better and introduce you to new colors you wind up loving, but might not otherwise have purchased. Many palettes are released as holiday gift sets, so keep your eyes peeled in January when they go on sale. These sale items are profit goldmines for makeup artists.

Consolidate Colors

Once you decide which foundation formulas you will keep in your kit, your next step is to choose the colors you will carry. There is absolutely no reason to carry every color in the line when colors can be blended. Generally, you can color match any face using only four or five shades.

Learning to mix foundations to match a face will be a profit maximizer for you. No brand of foundation out there works for everyone, so it's important to carry more than one formula. Becoming an ace color matcher will enable you to do this with just a handful of shades.

During makeup artistry seminars, I have personally seen inside the kits of some of the world's top makeup artists, and I can tell you that they do not have the space for each shade of foundation in every line they carry.

Top pros often have five or more different foundation formulas in their kit at any time, so it would be much too heavy and inefficient to stock each color. This also applies to concealers, color correctors, and most liquid and cream products. Less really *is* more.

Lip Glosses

The squeezable types of lip gloss are another money saver. Steer clear of packaging that requires you to dip into the bottle with a wand. As a busy artist and diligent practitioner of proper sanitation, you won't have time to continuously dip the wand into the tube looking for product to then scrape onto your palette, squeezable glosses are purposed to save you both time and money.

CHAPTER 33: Expanding Your Team

Even the most independent of makeup professionals needs occasional help from other talented artists. The last thing you want is to be forced to turn down a large bridal party because it is more than you can handle on your own.

Having a few people to call when large bridal parties come your way will help put more money in your pocket and can get you out of a bind in an emergency. The benefits of an "on call" team can go far beyond the financial rewards of being able to take on large parties. What if you are injured or sick and unable to make it to the job?

These worst-case scenarios happen more often than you'd think. You can't plan to avoid them, but you *can* have a plan for who you will call when the unexpected happens.

What to Look For In A Team Member

One of the best parts of being your own boss is getting to choose the people you work with. There is nothing more comforting than to have the support of a familiar face nearby during the intense moments of getting a bridal party ready for a wedding.

When the time to decide who you want on your beauty team comes, three things are essential:

First and foremost, choose someone you enjoy working with who treats your clients like his or her own. You need to be comfortable putting your name on their artistry skills. That means the quality of their work must be as high as your own. After all it is *you* the bride hired.

Above all else, your team members must be extremely reliable. When it comes to someone's wedding day, there is no room for people you can't rely on to be there when it counts. Each day on the job as a wedding stylist carries a much bigger responsibility than going to work at a beauty counter at the mall. Your team needs to clearly understand this.

Nobody come to mind right now? Don't be afraid to publish a job posting online via Craigslist. It's possible to find many talented artists to work with this way. Just make sure your job posting clearly lays out the objectives of the job and describes what you are looking for.

Tip: Ask responders to take specific steps when they reply to your posting. This simple trick will help you instantly weed out people who don't follow directions well.

How to Form A Professional Relationship
In the beginning, you may want to keep things informal and just work with new people on an as-needed basis. Lay out the details of the job very clearly, including what time they need to be there, how many people they will be working with, how much you will be paying them and method of payment.

Keep everything in writing via email. That way, they have a clear, quick reference when it's time to do the job. Often, you will be hired many months in advance of a wedding, and your team members need to have the details handy when the wedding day finally arrives.

If you find yourself working with a specific artist regularly and want to formalize the relationship, you may want to consider hiring an attorney to create a contractor agreement on your behalf. This agreement will define their role with your company, what is expected of them, and what you offer in return.

Be Clear About Their Role
This may be the first time you've been the boss, so it's important to make sure your team members clearly know their role with your company, both during and after the job.

For instance, will you allow them to use photos of work they do with your company for their own purposes? Will you allow them to seek reviews or receive referrals from your clients?

Part of being a business owner is managing people and protecting your company's assets. After all, you worked your tail off to build your business, so you have every right to set boundaries that ensure your own success.

CHAPTER 34: Reaching Your Goals

Likely, you've been hearing about the importance of setting personal goals since you were a small child. Writing down your goals may sound a bit cliché, but there really are very powerful reasons to do so – and to do it regularly. In fact, it's hard to think of examples of any successful makeup artists who got to where they are by chance or talent alone.

Each of us is responsible for our own fortunes or failures, and a vital part of building success is setting goals and holding yourself accountable for attaining your dreams. If you intend to build the life you want, you have to define what that would look like. I encourage you to buy a specific notebook for the sole purpose of mapping out your path to success and describing how you will achieve your goals.

To keep up with this regularly, you should have a combination of short-term, mid-range and long-term goals to keep you steadily focused on where your business is at any given time and where you want it to go. Make goals for this week, this month, six months and one year from now.

If you'd like to set goals farther out, do whatever feels right for you, but consider that your long-term goals may change as your plan evolves. Keep it focused by limiting long-term goals to just one year from now.

You'll get the most benefit out of the time you put into mapping out your goals if you don't let the process become a mundane to-do list. Instead, concentrate on aspirations you *know* are within reach if you work hard enough for them.

Whatever your personal goals may be, keep them in front of you as constant reminders of your own vision for success. Write Post-It notes on the mirror if it will help keep you motivated.

As a self-employed makeup artist, no one but you is in a position to hold yourself accountable for achieving success. The weight of being self-motivated and firmly in possession of the mental grit to make it through tough times is on your own shoulders.

By defining where you'd like to be and how you are going to get there, you greatly amplify the probability that you will achieve the milestones on your chosen path through life.

CHAPTER 35: Thinking Beyond Your Labor

The world's top makeup and hair stylists have a few things in common. Beyond being incredibly hard working, they build the right relationships and know how to leverage their following to increase their wealth.

As a novice artist, the most rewarding feeling is to be busy with clients who've hired you for your expertise and ability to turn any woman into a version of herself that is ten times more beautiful than before she sat in your chair. This may feel like the ultimate in success, but even those who love what they do eventually grow weary of endless hours on their feet.

Building a long-lasting career for yourself demands that you think beyond working with clients and create other ways to make money that don't require you to personally show up for each day's work. What does this concept refer to?

Implore yourself to start thinking of ways to expand your artistry that do not involve working directly with clients. Commonly thought of as passive streams of income, this is the key to success for your business – and your personal longevity.

There is no mystery in the fact that most makeup artists you encounter are in their 20s and 30s. Yes, this age group *is* dialed into the latest beauty trends, but the truth is that working on your feet is a hard job.

For that reason, it's vital to conjure up ways to leverage your talents that will put money in your pocket without breaking a sweat.

Potential Revenue Streams for Expansion
Are you finding yourself receiving requests from multiple brides who are all tying the knot on the same day? It's nearly impossible to

do more than one wedding per day because most bridal parties need to be beautified in the same timeframe. What a shame to turn down all of that additional business.

One solution for this dilemma is to build a beauty team that can do the actual work with bridal parties without you personally lifting a brush. As the owner of the company, you would handle communications with the bride, contracts and scheduling while your team members do all the styling.

The best part about this business model is that when *they* make money *you* make money. It is a great system that lets you maintain control of your company without having to be present at every wedding and do all the work yourself.

Refer to Chapter 33 on hiring team members and make sure to have a solid contractor agreement in place.

While your team does all of the hands-on work, you are ultimately responsible for the quality of their styling because it is your company the bride has hired. For this reason, it is essential that your team be comprised of trustworthy stylists who impress you with their skill, professionalism and ability to handle the pressures of the job.

If you can build the right artist lineup, this arrangement is incredibly rewarding. Plus, it allows you serve more brides than you ever could on your own.

The more brides coming your way, the greater potential for new reviews and exposure to larger audiences. You then have the option to roll those extra profits into more advertising – bringing even more brides your way. Total domination of your market? Why not!

Hair Accessories and Extensions
One of your brides' most common questions will be about clip-in hair extensions and where they can purchase bridal hair accessories. The available options may seem plentiful, but you would be surprised how uninformed brides are on this topic.

A selection of gorgeous hair accessories could be a very lucrative revenue stream for you. If you are the crafty type, you could make some of them yourself. Otherwise, search online for affordable wholesale products that you can then mark up and sell to your clients.

Mobile Tanning and Lash Extensions
Spray tanning is rapidly gaining in popularity as women become more aware of the dangers of baking in the sun. Many makeup artists recommend brides get a spray tan before their wedding day, not so much to make them tan but to even out their overall skin tone.

There is nothing worse than a picture of a bride with obvious tan lines on her chest or a blotchy neck that is a completely different color than her face. Spray tan formulas have come a long way since the days when they made women look like orange Barbie dolls.

It's nearly effortless to point out to brides all the benefits, including the ease of hiring you to come to their house to perform a custom spray tan in the days leading up to the wedding.

Lash extensions are also gaining in popularity as more women learn about the benefits of waking up every day with a full set of voluminous lashes. Extensions are much longer lasting than classic strip lashes and make a bride's eyes look beautiful for all the photos taken in the days leading up to her wedding.

The great thing about all of these add-on products is that they require very little hard-pitched selling from you. All you really have to do is talk about the benefits and what you like about tanning, extensions, etc.

Remember, brides are spending more money on their wedding day than on any other day of their lives, and they are constantly seeking more ways to make the day memorable and appear drop-dead-gorgeous in those wedding photos.

YouTube and Social Media
If you enjoy being in front of the camera, you can reach a limitless

audience by sharing your knowledge via YouTube, Pinterest and other forms of social media.

For every bride who hires you, there exists a virtually endless number of women out there who are tasked with doing their own hair and makeup for their weddings. These women are seeking guidance in droves via YouTube videos and Pinterest tutorials every single day.

The perks of sharing your knowledge via social media go well beyond building a large audience for your brand to include the potential for Google ad revenue deposited directly into your bank account.

Social media has never been more exciting. It is amazing to be able to reach people all over the world, boosting self-confidence by simply guiding them with what you already know.

I challenge you to think of new ways to grow your business and share your passions for beauty. Show the world what you can do and you never know who you will inspire.

ABOUT THE AUTHOR

Theresa Amundsen is a freelance makeup artist and lover of all things beauty. She is a graduate of The Fashion Institute of Design & Merchandising in Los Angeles with a degree in Beauty Industry Merchandising & Marketing.

Theresa lives in San Diego, California, and enjoys educating and inspiring others to succeed on their own terms and live the life they have imagined.

Printed in Great Britain
by Amazon.co.uk, Ltd.,
Marston Gate.